Cherubim and Flaming Sword

by

W.B. Godbey

First Fruits Press
Wilmore,
Kentucky
c2018

ISBN: 9781621718093…

Cherubim and flaming sword.
By W.B. Godbey. © 2018
First Fruits Press, © 2018
Digital version at http://place.asburyseminary.edu/firstfruitsheritagematerial/…

For all other uses, contact:

First Fruits Press
B.L. Fisher Library
Asbury Theological Seminary
204 N. Lexington Ave.
Wilmore, KY 40390
http://place.asburyseminary.edu/firstfruits

Godbey, W. B. (William Baxter), 1833-1920.
    Cherubim and flaming sword / by W.B. Godbey. – Wilmore, KY : First
Fruits Press, ©2018.

        pages ; cm.

        Reprint. Previously published: Nashville, Tennessee : Pentecostal Mission
    Publishing Company, 1917.
    ISBN: 9781621718093 (pbk.)

        1. Sanctification. 2. Holiness. I. Title.

BT767.G62 2018   234.8

Cover design by Haley Hill

asburyseminary.edu
800.2ASBURY
204 North Lexington Avenue
Wilmore, Kentucky 40390

First Fruits
THE ACADEMIC OPEN PRESS OF ASBURY SEMINARY

First Fruits Press
The Academic Open Press of Asbury Theological Seminary
204 N. Lexington Ave., Wilmore, KY 40390
859-858-2236
first.fruits@asburyseminary.edu
asbury.to/firstfruits

CHERUBIM AND FLAMING SWORD

By REV. W. B. GODBEY

Author of many books on
Bible Holiness

1917

Pentecostal Mission Publishing Company
Nashville, Tennessee

BENSON PRINTING CO., NASHVILLE

CONTENTS

Cherubim and Flaming Sword

CHAPTER I

CHERIBINA

This is a Hebrew word in the plural number. A cherub is a very high order of archangel, and the word in the Bible, especially as used by Isaiah and Ezekiel, denotes the divine presence. Isaiah (6th chapter). A juvenile prophet was permitted to behold the glory of the Lord filling the temple. His presence demonstrated by the cloud, flooding it and setting the columns, in the colonnade, all around a jar with the momentum of His sublime presence; Seraphim on their pinions above shouting aloud, "Who will go for us?" The young man, though not yet sanctified, could stand it no longer, and shouted aloud, "Here am I, send me, though I am a man of unclean lips."

God is so scarce of people in this world who will let Him have His way with them that He refuses none, even Mary Magdalene, out of whom John cast seven demons, whom John Wesley believed to be a public prostitute, when she was willing to let the Lord take her and make what He would out of her, He not only accepted her, gloriously converted her, but honored her with the front of the feminine wing of His apostolic ministry. She was last at the cross, first at the sepulchre, and first to receive the full orbed commission, "Go and preach the risen Savior to a lost world."

So God accepted the unsanctified Hebrew prophet, sending an angel at once with a live coal from heaven's altar, to lay it on his lip and take his sin away, *i. e.*, 800 years antecedently, gave him the Pentecostal baptism with the Holy Ghost and fire to sanctify him wholly. Thus He gave him the basal qualification to go to the ends of the earth preaching the everlasting gospel, with the Holy Ghost sent down from heaven. This seraphic call is still ringing around the world, "Who will go for us?" Reader, be sure you say yes, regardless of your qualification, because the Lord is ready with His omnipotent grace, freely to supply all your deficiencies.

These Seraphims each had six wings; "with twain they did cover their faces, with twain they did cover their feet, and with twain they did fly." Here you see the outfit we need to accept the urgent call. God is ringing in our ears. "The harvest is great and the laborers are few," and at the same time He importunes us to pray God to send more laborers into His vineyard. This day a thousand million heathen, longing for something better than their wood and stone gods who cannot do anything for them, reach out their hands and cry, "Come over and help us."

We see that one pair of the wings is to cover our faces, thus beautifully and forcefully symbolizing humility, which John Fletcher, the great exponent of Methodism, pronounced the most important Christian grace. When interrogated, "What is the most important grace?," he answers "Humility; when asked what was next, he said "Humility." They proceeded to ask the third and fourth time, and he said "Humility" all the time. The inquirer desisted, having received the overwhelming verdict in favor of the conclusion that humility was the pre-eminent Christian grace.

This perfect humility puts us down on the bottom of the valley of humiliation, whence there is no falling, as there is no place into which we can fall. We actually have in our experience fulfilled the grand Calvinistic dogma, so much coveted by all pilgrims for glory bound, *i. e.*, the final perseverance of the saints.

Satan uses this dogma to send millions into hell who neither know nor have grace, or had it and lost it, solacing them with the delusion, "once in grace, always in grace." Perfect humility really solves the problem, giving them the *sine qua non* to which they all aspire and no failure about it. Therefore, go for perfect humility down on the bottom of the valley of humiliation. Stay there and you have nothing to do but shout victory forever.

John Fletcher was a popular pastor in the high Church of England at Madeley and had heard so much evil report about the Methodists as fanatical disturbers of the churches, that he was prejudiced, and still he was electrified with curiosity to see them. Passing by an old barn in the field, he heard very loud singing and asked the driver what it meant, and he said they were Methodists. They had driven them out of all the churches and they were holding their meetings in dilapidated buildings and under green trees. John Wesley even was closed out of the church his father had served a solid generation, but preached to the spellbound multitudes standing on his father's tombstone, which he erected with his own money. It belonged to him and they could not keep him off it.

Then Fletcher said to the coachman that he had heard so much about them and had never seen them, and he would like so much to stop and go in a little while. The coachman responded that he was in the same fix, and they dismounted to go into the meeting. It fixed the destiny of Fletcher forever, as the light broke into his heart and he saw to his astonishment that he had never been born from above. His conviction was so pungent that he let the coach go on and stayed with those poor despised Methodists till very soon he became one himself, not only gloriously converted, but powerfully sanctified. He was naturally timid and the law did not protect public worship like it does now. They not only threw mud on the preachers, but beat and stoned them, apparently with impunity, giving suspicion that the clergy had encouraged the mob thus to cruelly persecute God's people.

John Wesley was naturally brave and consequently he was hated, mobbed, and beaten. On one occasion, preaching on the street, the mob assaulted him, throwing rocks and knocking out all of the lights, they seized the preacher and dragging him away into a back alley they beat him until they thought he was dead; laconically solacing themselves, "I reckon the old canterum (a nickname they had given him through reproach) will not bleat any more." They left him in his blood, on the bosom of mother earth, until day, and God gave him that beautiful hymn in the Methodist collection:

"Shall Simon bear the cross alone and all the world
        go free,
  No, there is a cross for everyone, and that takes
      in me."

Thus he exhibited the meek and lowly spirit of an angel utterly unretaliatory.

On another occasion the mob dragged him away and threw him into the river Thames, running through London, and he said he had not the slightest fear of drowning. All he thought about was some important papers which he had in his pocket, and the water would ruin them. While Wesley was so brave, as to never flicker from his testimony, come what might, Fletcher's native timidity, more like a woman than a man, caused him to flicker from the awful persecution and withhold his testimony till he lost his experience four times. He found it so difficult to get it back, that having received it in God's wonderful mercy the fifth time, he settled forever the problem of testimony by roaring it out in his daily peregrinations regardless of consequences.

Therefore we should all profit by his collapse, which gave him so much trouble as he always believed that the true remedy was bold testimony led by the Spirit, without a flicker even amid howling demons, raging policemen, roaring mobs, rotten eggs flying through the air, which smell sweet for Jesus.

In a camp-meeting in Texas, they pelted me so with eggs as to knock my hat to pieces, so it would not stay on my head, and deluge my clothing from top to toe. At the close of the meeting, when I went to town seven miles to take the train, and the merchants had found it out and heard the mighty works the Lord did on the campground, multitudes saved and sanctified, old grudges settled with showers of perfect love, the salvation wave rolling over the place like a mighty sea, they quarreled with each other for the privilege of dressing me at their own cost. I found it necessary to compromise the matter by dividing up, taking some from one and some from another. I concluded in the finale that the devil had overshot himself.

My clothing was old and well nigh spent, but it was superseded by a new suit. I will never forget the face of the leader of that mob as I saw the devil in his physiognomy big as a rhinoceros in him. He was coming very near me and throwing the eggs in my face with all violence, knocking my spectacles whirling. I cried to God to save his soul and call him to preach, that he might blow the silver trumpet while I played on the golden harp.

The answer to the prayer was wonderful, as a thunderboldt struck his heart, putting on him a conviction which never let up, but got worse, though he came back to the camp no more. It downed him fortunately among Free Methodists, who prayed him through, not only into the kingdom, but joyfully into Beulah Land, where he gladly took his gospel trumpet and began to blow. I afterwards D., V., succeeded him in a Free Methodist camp-meeting, in St. Louis, where he told all of his experience. He went to China a missionary and when I was preaching there eleven years ago, I was anxious to visit him and help him in his labor of love. But Boxer troubles, their killing the missionaries, the rulers of the country would not permit me to go to him, and I had to content myself to preach in the cities where they could protect me.

"With twain he did cover his feet." This is the experience of purity, as the feet are down in the mud, and consequently the recipients of the major pollution, incidental to life's journey. These angels protect their feet with their wings so they remain perfectly clean, and just ready to tread the Brussel carpets of celestial mansions.

The Cherubim is the symbol of the divine presence which cannot brook the slightest impurity, beautifully contrary of the transcendent Pauline standard we find conspicuous in all his writings. We are sometimes demanded Paul's testimony to sanctification. It is like the giant who had a hundred hands and Argus with his hundred eyes, and Cerberus, Pluto's dog, who had three dog heads parallel in front, and one hundred snake heads all over his body, rendering his personality invisible, as myth certifies. He would lie in the shed while souls were coming through the gate into hell, but if any tried to get out they would never try it but once. 2 Cor. 1:12, "We have been with you in holiness and the purity of God," not as (E. V.) "simplicity and godly sincerity." Those words are taken from the Latin, and in that language mean entire sanctification, simplicity little signifying purity. The Greek for godly sincerity is *eilekrinia,* from *eiles,* a sunbeam, and *kri nwo,* to judge, and consequently signifying judged, in the sunbeam, which reveals every atom of impurity. We little children in our log house in the mountain home would see the sunbeam as it appeared above the horizon enter the room through the missing chink in the wall, and show the dust in the air, so conspicuously as it waved up and down and to and fro in the morning breeze and we would shout, "Gogle!"

Rest assured when the great Son of Righteousness illuminates you here He will reveal every part of impurity identified with the residuum of depravity, which Father Wesley certifies is abiding in every human heart. Our wonderful Savior proposes to make it so clean, by the elixir of His own precious blood, that God's own eye never discovers a solitary atom.

The papacy is really the progeny of the bottomless pit, as it is the antichrist of prophecy, abundantly evidenced in the infallible word. Rev., 13th ch., we see the beast rise up out of the sea with seven heads and ten horns. You observe the source of this beast, the people of this world who are all fallen in Adam and redeemed in Christ are in the prophecies, constantly symbolized by the sea, which when calm, beautifully typifies the people resting in peace and prosperity. In the storm it vividly symbolizes the people as in the old world this day, lacerated by revolutions, rushing furiously into deadly conflict, vieing with each other in the horrific work of man's slaughter; deluging mother earth with the blood of her own sons, which she drinks coercively with sighs and groans, heaping her bosom with mountains of the dead.

Rome, founded by Romulus 573, B.C., was first a kingdom 253 years, when she plunged headlong into bloody revolutions, out of which eventually she arose a republic, and so remained five hundred years. Universal wreckage amid seas of blood and horrors indescribable, culminated in the hopeless downfall of the republic; once more rising out of a bloody sepulchre, a universal empire. Augustus Cæsar, in his golden house, looked out on five thousand Senators, living in silver houses, constituting his council board of his administration of every nation beneath the skies, his crown was radiant with the rays of an unsetting sun and her sceptre swept the circumference of the globe. The temple of Janus, which opened, signified war, and closed, recognizing peace with all the world, at that time closed for the good reason that every nation bowed the knee to haughty Rome, leaving no enemy in all the earth. This was the third closing of the temple, transpiring during the reign of the first king of Rome and the second following the first Punic war, which lasted a hundred and forty years.

The reign of Augustus was memoralized by the most wonderful event of all the ages, the birth of our Savior, which had to be postponed, till Rome conquered all the world and peace universally reigned, as He is the Prince of Peace. The generations had been waiting more than four thousand years, praying, crying and sighing for the long expected Messiah, when sure enough the shepherds of Bethlehem are saluted by the shouts of the angels hovering over them:

"Hark a glad voice the lonely desert cheers,
    Prepare the way, a God, a God appears!
    Lo! earth receives Him from the bending skies;
    Sink down ye mountains, ye valleys rise!
    With heads declined ye did homage pay!
    Be smooth ye rocks, ye rapid floods,
    Give way, the Savior comes!
    By ancient bards foretold,
    Hear Him, ye deaf, and all ye blind behold!"

God makes the wrath of man to praise Him and restrains the remainder of wrath, i. e., when it will not praise Him He stops it altogether.

See how wondefully he utilized those 753 years of Roman conquest to establish universal peace for the advent of His Son. A consolidated universal monarchy was the very thing for the evangelization of all the world. The apostles went to the ends of the earth, all preaching heroically till bloody martyrdom liberated them for their upward flight, to join the blood-washed millions, from Abel down through the stormy centuries, culminating on the bloody height of Calvary. Rome was an empire in the day of Christ and the apostles, the sixth head of the beast; as during her stormy revolutions she was for a time a triumvirate, ruled by three men, and at another time a tribuneship, ruled by the Chiliarchs; at another a dictatorship, ruled by one man, this making the Papacy the seventh head of the beast.

As we see, this beast came up out of the sea, *i. e.*, emanated from the fallen, depraved people, and was consequently the minion of Satan. Another beast, the eleventh, came up out of the earth, with two horns like a lamb, and yet he spoke as the dragon. This is the ecclesiastical hemisphere of the carnal globe, symbolized by the marine beast. Daniel says that one horn was much higher than the other, though it came up last, the short horn thus typifying Greek Catholicism and the long horn the Roman, though younger than the Greek, was so much larger, 275 millions, while the Greek Church has only 125 millions. Both were long ago captured and manipulated by Satan, and this day his right arm in all the earth, the old harlot mother of prophecy, whose daughter we sadly find in all the Protestant Churches, all of which are destined to go down in the tribulation (Rev. 18th chapter) with all carnal ecclesiasticisms, to rise no more forever.

They will be superseded by the Holiness churches, destined to fill the world with the ingress of the millennium, and abide forever. The Pope is the seventh head of both the marine and tarine beasts, and the antichrist of the latter day prophecies, which we see abundantly confirmed (Rev., 17th chapter). Where you see the bejeweled harlot mounted on the bloody dragon, to the unutterable astonishment of the prophet, and no wonder, because when he saw the bride of Christ, (12th ch.) she was fleeing from the bloody Dragon after her to eat up her child, and now what a paradoxical change! She has not only compromised with the dragon, but is riding him, *i. e.,* the poor weak church instead of running for life and suffering martyrdom at the hand of a Satan-ridden world has compromised with it, receiving its money, honor and glory. She has changed by fatal apostacy from the pure bride of Christ, to that of antichrist, and is consequently the harlot of Babylon, so appalling in all the prophecies.

Rev., 17th ch., exhibits the fallen bride mounted on the scarlet beast (the world), glittering with jewelry, pomp, pagantry and phantasmagoria from top to toe; the animal taking a kicking up spell and throwing him over her head and eating him up without mercy verified in the extensive revolt of the secular powers against the papacy, A.D. 1870. Pope Pius IX constrained the Vatican councils of 535 bishops with the hierarchies to vote his infallibility, despite the awful thunderstorm God sent to wrap the Campus Martuis in midnight at noonday. The ink was scarcely dry when Victor Emmanuel, King

of Sardina, entered Rome with his army and shook
him down from his triple temporal throne, Lom-
bards, Astrogoths, and Ravenna. The Catholic
armies were never able to regain them, as Garibaldi
defeated them and the people erected a monument to
his memory and another on the other side com-
memorative of Victor Emmanuel at the cost of
$11,000,000. The governments throughout the
Catholic world repudiated the Papistical authority
and confiscated princely fortunes of their property
in all parts of 'he world.

The reason .e know that the pope is the antichrist, is the simple fact that anti means instead of,
and the pope has always claimed to be the vicar of
Christ and the vice regent of God, and to have authority over all the kings of the earth corroborated
by the positive stated in this chapter that the antichrist will be the eighth head of the beast and
one of the seven. It is a well-known historic fact
that the pope is the seventh head of the beast, the
other six having all passed away; the empire under
which our Savior and His apostles spent their lives
having fallen with Rome A.D. 476, leaving the
papacy the only surviving head. Consequently as
the antichrist is the eighth head of the beast the
pope is the identical and unmistakable character.

When Daniel 7:9 is fulfilled, "I beheld till the
thrones were cast down, and the Ancient of Days did
sit and a fiery stream went before Him and a thousand thousand ministered unto Him." (*i. e.*, a million
destroying angels will come down with God the
Father in the fulfillment of the promise of the Father to His ascended and glorified Son, that He should
rule this world without a rival forever.)

The tribulation will be simply a united effort on the part of all the kings to regain the thrones from which God has taken them for the occupancy of His Son in the fulfillment of His promise. The pope from the beginning has claimed the right to rule the world as the viceregent of God and the vicar of Christ, when the kings all fall. (Quite a lot of them have fallen already (1917) and all the rest are rickety and shaking as by the throes of an earthquake.) Then the fallen kings in their desperation will recognize His supremacy as a drowning man catches at a straw and continue that recognition till you see them all go down in blood, 19th ch., the last of the secular powers. An angel stands on the sun and calling vociferously to all the carniverous beasts and birds to rally to the grand carnival and feast at the royal banquet of queens, princes, potentates and their armies, leaving their bones unburied. The Pope and Mohammed are both caught away alive and hurried into the lake of fire a thousand years before the devil ever gets there.

The papacy is the carnal beast of prophecy, the antichrist of the tribulation and Catholicism. The harlot of Babylon so prominent in the Johannic prophecies and really Satan's broad, slick plank over which he is sliding multiplied millions into hell. This priestcraft authenticates a sinning religion; drunkards and harlots are in full fellowship in their churches, vainly looking to the priest to forgive their sins for filthy lucre with the distinct understanding that they go on unblushingly and commit the same sins over and over. They sink deeper and deeper into iniquity; at the same time vainly hallucinated

2

with the fond delusion that they are going to heaven, when on a bee line to hell through the church. They depend on their besotted priests to take their sins away, themselves the worst sinners in all the world.

The pope claims Holiness as an official title and is so recognized by the whole Catholic world. They not only look to him as the incarnation of holiness, but actually recognize him as a god; thus plunging headlong into gross idolatry. Not only do they worship the Virgin Mary, all the apostles and all the archangels, Gabriel and Michael, but actually worship their living ministry so abominable in the sight of God, who throughout the Bible calls idolatry an abomination. Not only the 450,000,000 Catholics 1,000,000,000 pagans and 300,000,000 Mohammedans, all deep down in idolatry, but the great Protestant churches are on their track, moving at race horse speed.

Romans, 1st ch., the first departure from God is into intellectualism, i. e., mentalities instead of spiritualities. All true religion is spirituality pure and uncontaminated with materialities or mentalities. The second stage is idolatry, including the 1,650,-000,000 above mentioned, of whom so many are really in brutality and devil worship.

This leaves a tremendous work for the comparatively few holiness people to evangelize these teeming millions, who envelop the globe in the sable winding sheets of everlasting woe; thus populating hell so rapidly and copiously. What an awful pity when damnation is a sheer gratuity, Jesus has naturally paid the debt, having satisfied the violated law, brought life and immortality to light. None of these hellward bound millions have anything to do but

leave the devil and sin world without end and give
Jesus a chance to save them. At the same time He
actually gives them a heaven on earth instead of
the awful stygian prelude, in which Satan's people
suffer a thousand deaths and then die in misery long
before their time.

All the people in the world are anxious to go to
heaven, but the trouble is the fallen prophets, Satan's preachers, are on all sides to hoax, stultify and
delude them with a sinning religion, but in every
case, like Dives (Luke 15th ch.), they will lift up
their eyes in hell tormented by the devouring flame
through all eternity. Hell is so awful that it is horrific to think of ever going hither; yet the fact that
we never can get away is infinitely more appalling
than even the flames of hell. We might endure them
a season if there was any hope of deliverance. The
Catholics all offer them sanctification in the fires of
purgatory, which is only a devil's hell. It would
have sanctified the devil and all his myrmidons long
ago if such a thing were possible. The overwhelming
majority of Protestants preach sanctification in
death. This is an utter delusion, as sanctification
is a pure spirituality, which physical death does not
effect in any way and cannot.

Oh, how we need all the holy people in the world
to go and tell the deluded multitudes about Jesus,
who is everything they need; not only ready, willing
and waiting omnipresent with every lost soul on the
globe, but needing no help whatever to save any one.
The great trouble is Satan's false prophets throng
the whole earth and head off Jesus in His love and
mercy omnipotent to save; shoving off on the people their priestcraft water baptism, and diversified

churchisms, all Satanic manipulations to keep them from coming directly to the "Lamb of God, who taketh away the sin of the world." John 1:9. Thus these false prophets, two million Catholic priests, augmented by Campbellite preachers, Mormon prohpets, and so many unconverted preachers, even in orthodox churches, having salvation in their creed, but destitute of it in their own hearts, cannot preach what they have not.

The Roman Catholic commentator, Lignori, denounces the doctrine of purity and execrates it with the bitterest anathemas. The abominable doctrine of purity has given the Catholic Church more trouble than anything else. How awful for people to have such leaders and teachers, the sworn emissaries of the bottomless pit, manipulated by the devil to deceive the multitude and lead them to hell. The doctrine of purity is actually *the doctrine* of the Bible; everything else simply the chicanery of Satan under the cognomen of Bible truth in order to deceive the people and lead them to hell. Holiness, *i. e.*, entire sanctification, as God never goes partnership with the devil, is the only doctrine in the Bible, shining and shouting from Alpha to Omega; not only flooding the blessed old Book, but run over on the outside. You see on every one superscribed "Holy Bible," which simply means that the Bible is a book on Holiness, with nothing else. The reason why you need all my books (this is the 223d) is the simple fact that they are all Bible teachers and nothing else. The brightest and best preachers on the globe by speech and pen say that they learn more out of them than any others. Every one of them tells you the sure way to heaven by the grand old route of the supernatural birth and entire sanctification, absolutely infallible, as God built up this highway of Holiness every step from the city of Destruction to the New Jerusalem, "no lion or ravenous beast," nor tollgate on it. It is perfectly free for all the vilest of the vile, having nothing to do but tip his hat to the devil, dash off at race horse speed and run with ever accelerated velocity till he leaps through the pearly gates and receives a starry crown never to fade away, but to receive new lustre through the flight of eternal ages.

"With the third pair of wings he did fly." Hence you see locomotion prominent in the sanctified experience, as the commission "go" as well as preach. We must always be ready to go, as Jesus said, a prophet was without honor in his own country. We see this fact potently illustrated in His family who did not believe on him. We are astonished over their unbelief in His Messiaship, while they believed most earnestly that He was not only a prophet, but the greatest prophet who had ever been on the earth, as His miracles acceded all His predecessors.

We must remember that Elijah and Elisha had filled that whole country with miracles, actually raising the dead to life. I stood at 10 A.M. on the spot where Jesus resurrected the son of the widow at Nain, and the same day at 2 P.M. on the opposite side of Little Mount Hermon, where Elisha raised the son of the Shulenintish woman. The reason why none of His brothers believed He was the Christ is because it is very hard for us to believe great things about home folks. For this reason you see the importance of leaving home to preach the Gospel.

Reader, I take it for granted you have all ready said yes to the call to preach, which is ringing in the ears of all the sanctified people. From the fact that the 1,700,000,000 populating this world can only command a little crowd of saved people, who alone are competent to tell others how to get saved, all imperatively need to carry the bread of heaven and the water of life to the perishing millions famishing wheresoever we turn our eyes. Let no one say, I have no traveling money. Our Savior never used any, but walked everywhere except over the sea, where doubtless His disciples paid His fare. He never carried money; illustrated when in Capernium they called on Him and Peter to pay their temple assessment, a coin of 30 cents, He had to send Peter to the sea to throw in a hook and catch a fish, in whose mouth he found stater (a coin of sixty cents) sufficient to pay for them both.

Walking is much more hygienical than riding, and we should all start out in the track of our great Captain, walking till God's providence picks us up and gives us a ride. I have been preaching sixty-four years, beginning a pedestrian, then an equestrian, culminating in my commission given by my presiding Bishop to evangelize the whole world thirty-three years ago. Under this I traveled four times around the historic world, preaching in Europe, Asia, and Africa, crossed this continent, riding the iron horse, over sea and land, costing me a princely fortune, which God gave me as I needed it, because I began without a penny.

When you get sanctified wholly you say yes to the Holy Ghost all the time, who gives you the wings by which you fly to the ends of the earth, regardless of towering mountains lifting their blue summits far above the clouds, thundering seas, and stormy oceans. Where there is a will there is a way. When people do not go and preach, the conclusion follows that they have never received the Cherubic wings, and they should tarry in the upper room till the fire baptism descends from heaven and gives them the pinions, competent to carry them as on eagle wings to the ends of the earth. Therefore, if you have not the locomotive pinions, remember, God has them for you. This wonderful salvation is as free as the air we breathe and the waters of the limpid rill which flows down the majestic hill, sparkling, leaping and bounding, expediting its flights to the beautiful crystal sea.

Therefore, we are all left without excuse. Ethiopian hands longingly reach out and beckon us to come, while the cry, "do come over and help us," rings in our ears. Acts, 16th ch., reads. I hope your affirmative response has already reached the throne, as in the case of the youthful Hebrew prophet. Isaiah, 6th ch., "Here am I Lord, send me, but I am a man of unclean lips, i. e., not sanctified. In this wonderful age of free grace for all who will receive it, it leaves no apology for the damnation of a solitary soul.

In this succession of the Hebrew prophet, this moment answer in the affirmative, resting assured that God will receive you and give you Cherub pinions to fly around the world, honored above the angels to preach the Gospel to the lost millions and receive a starry crown, which will never fade away, but accumulate new luster through the flights of endless ages.

CHAPTER II

FLAMING TORCH

Heb. 4:12. We have the positive statement that this sword is simply the word of God, and that it has two edges. The salvation edge is keen as lighting, and absolutely sure to cut forever out of your immortal spirit all the disharmony with God, which Satan transmitted to every son and daughter of Adam's ruined race, "Lord I am vile, conceived in sin, born unholy and unclean, sprung from the man whose guilty fall corrupts his race and ruins all."

Psalms 51:5 clearly proclaims the great fundamental doctrine of total depravity hereditary in every human spirit, and only expurgated by the wonderful efficacy of the cleansing blood. This is the omnipotent elixir of entire sanctification, administered by the Holy Spirit to every soul, fully abandoned to God for this world and all others.

"Here I give my all to thee,
    Friends and time and earthly store,
Soul and body Thine to be,
    Wholly Thine forevermore.

"Wash me in the precious blood,
    Cleanse me in the purifying flood,
Lord, I give to Thee my life and all to be,
    Thine henceforth forevermore."

The blessed Holy Spirit is grieved by your perilous postponement of this *sine qua non* of our own admission into heaven. Remember, "procrastina-

tion is the thief of time." There is not a soul in all
the regions of hopeless despair who ever expected to
make his bed in hell. He simply postponed till the
golden opportunities fled away; and the grim monster galloped upon his pale horse, lassoed him and
dragged him down to the dismal doom of the eternal damned.

This scripture certifies that the word of God is
"alive," *i. e.,* invested with the very life of God, and
actually sharper than any two-edged sword, cleaving
asunder soul and spirit, joints and marrow, *i. e.,*
a discerner of the thought and intents of the heart.
Man is a trinity, consisting of spirit (*pneuma*), soul
(*Psychee*), and body (*sooma*). 1 Thess. 5:23. All
religion is spirituality, whereas Satan does his utmost to destroy the work of the Holy Spirit, and
shove off on you mentalities. This is the trouble
with the popular churches, fine houses, pipe organs,
cushioned pews, gothic domes, Corinthian columns,
tall steeples, paid choirs, all mournful reminders of
the melancholy fact that the church is dead and
actually metamorphosed into a morgue. It is the
receptacle of dead bodies, instead of the barracks
of Emmanuel's army, marching forth under the
blood-stained banner to conquer the world for
Christ.

The human spirit is yourself, consisting of the
conscience, the will and the affections. This is the
media of conviction, regeneration and sanctification,
followed by glorification, when this mortal puts on
immortality. Without these mighty works there is
no salvation. The conscience is God's telephone,
through which he speaks to us. The will is the king
of humanity, and the medium of conversion, which

puts you where you say yes to God all the time, and no to the devil incessantly. The elements of the carnal mind are conquered in regeneration and kept down by triumphant grace. You have victory over temptation, and live free from condemnation because you commit no known sin.

This is a terrible civil war with the remainder of depravity still in the heart and prone to rise in the form of envy, jealousy, bigotry, prejudice, animosity, hatred, revenge, malice, covetousness, pride, vanity, lust, passion, temper, and all affections antagonistic to pure and perfect love. These must be expurgated by the blood, which the Holy Spirit applies when Jesus baptizes you. At the same time He burns up all the old man's furniture, along with sectarianism, idolatry in all its forms and phases, sorcery, witchcraft, and everything pertaining to Satan's kingdom.

He gives you a clean heart, so Satan fishes in vain in your pond. Nothing in you will nibble at his bait, gold, silver, houses, lands, affections, promotion or anything pertaining to this vain, vile world. Satan is on the throne and his false prophest are the popular preachers, singing the siren song of sinful pleasures, displaying all the pomp and every conceivable allurement. There are hell traps everywhere to catch the unsuspecting youth in the Satanic lasso; to lead him away and lull him to sleep by the charming melodies of enchantment. The vampire of irretrievable doom, stealthily, slipping in fatal proximity, inserts his soft tentacles through the pores of the skin and sucks the blood, thus filling his voracious stomach and leaving a lifeless corpse.

The baptism Jesus gives with the Holy Ghost and fire is the only remedy for the awful doom of damnation awaiting the whole human race. It was cunningly captured by Satan in his wonderful Eden victory, where God actually preached to Mother Eve that a son of hers would rise, conquer the devil, restore lost humanity and in glorious deeds would actually regain Paradise.

We are living in momentous times, when Satan is marshalling earth and hell, to populate the latter while he has a chance. He is using 2,000,000 Catholic priests, with Mormon prophets, and preachers of all cognomens, along with multitudes of pagan priests, under the guise of religion, transforming the world into a pandemonium. We remember our Savior's words, "Broad is the road that leads to death and thousands walk together there," while wisdom shows a narrow path, with here and there a traveler, despite the superabounding grace of God, in our wonderful Christ, perfectly free for every son and daughter of lost humanity.

With actually nothing to do but tip their hats to the devil and bid him an eternal farewell and to dash away at locomotive speed, for the King's highway of Holiness, Jesus builds it with his own bleeding hands, from the City of Destruction to the New Jerusalem. No lion nor ravenous beast on it, no tollgate (Isa., 35th ch.), and it is perfectly free for all.

O! why does not everyone move out on the highway? Be pilgrims bound for glory, singing jubilantly, "I am bound for the kingdom, will you go to glory with me?" My old companions, fare you well, I will not go with you to hell. If you will not go with me, we part company to meet no more, till we all stand before the great white throne. There we shall hear the King say to the sheep on the right, "Come ye blessed of my Father, inherit the kingdom prepared for you, before the foundation of the world;" and to the goats on the left, "Depart from me, ye cursed, into eternal fire prepared for the devil and his angels. These shall go away into eternal punishment and the righteous into eternal life."

Matt. 25:31, 46. This scripture reveals the final judgment of the heathen, who live and die, and never receive the literal gospel. This is confirmed in the fact that the sheep on the right, respond, "When saw we Thee hungry, thirsty, sick or in prison, and ministered not unto Thee?" Thus showing that they never had known Him historically, but had walked in all the light they had by their own conscience, God's telephone, the light of nature. The untutored in his primeval wilds sees God in the clouds and hears Him in the winds, whose soul proud science never taught to stray. As the solar walk, the milky way, the light of the Holy Spirit shines on every person coming into the world. John 1:9.

Every human soul who walks in every light he has, and is ready to walk in more light the moment God gives it, is saved and will be sanctified like all infants and idiots. It is done in the article of death, through the normal effiicacy of the great vicarious atonement Jesus made on Calvary for every human being ever born into the world through the flights of endless ages.

Meanwhile you see the goats, *i. e.,* the wicked, turned away on the left, sink into the unquenchable fires of an endless hell, because they did not these benefactions to the least of his brethren, *i. e.,* every human being. They lived like hogs and dogs for themselves alone, in counter-distinction to the sheep. They had been good and kind to every human being they ever met in life's journey.

This final judgment of the heathen is a sunburst of hope in behalf of the multiplied millions in all ages and nations, having lived and died without the written Gospel. We cannot say, without Christ, because the Holy Spirit was present (Gen. 1:2) before an inch of land was ever seen, while the earth was enveloped in a bankless ocean. "He was hovering over the face of the waters," i. e., forming the continent and islands, and has been in the world ever since. You must remember that He is the Spirit of Jesus. Acts 16:6-7.

Hence the idea that any person has ever lived on the earth without the wide open door of free salvation at his feet, and nothing to do but walk into it and shout the victory, is untrue. No soul can say in Judgment Day, "You gave me no chance for the salvation of my soul." The simple truth is that the free omnipotent grace of God in Christ actually reaches every human soul, far back in the prenatal state, the very moment soul and body united constituted personality. Heb. 2:9. By the grace of God Christ tasted death for every man, i. e., true reading, every human being. The Greek, huper patos, means, the very phraseology vicarious substitutionary atonement which the Lord made for every human being born of Adam's ruined race; thus making a glorious run on the devil, who captured us all seminally in Adam. (1 Cor. 15:22.) Jesus lassoes every human being personally the very moment soul and body united, constitute personality.

Thus the triumphantly consolatory conclusion, that all our babes are born Christians. You see it abundantly confirmed in the case of the prodigal son and his elder brother, who represent every human being ever born into the world. They were both born in the father's house, i. e., the kingdom of God; the junior, unfortunately straying away, i. e., backsliding, while his senior brother stayed at home, fat and flourishing all the time the prodigal was recklessly wasting his patrimony. He became an abject beggar, actually reaching the hog pen, the last station this side of hell. Fortunately grace prevailed and he bade adieu to all the comrades of his prodigal life and came home, lovingly reclaimed by the father's copious embrace and kiss. He was speedily sanctified when the best robe and the ring were put on him; called to preach when the shoes for his pedestrian circuit were brought.

The elder brother, on arrival, told his father that he had never transgressed his commandment, thus showing he had never forfeited his citizenship in the kingdom by apostacy. But he badly needed sanctfiication to take out of him all the fret and jealousy which he manifested. He felt grossly mistreated by the jubilant congratulations of his backslidden brother, and that all of the big shout roaring in that Holiness meeting ought to be over him, who had been so good, instead of his brother, who had actually brought disgrace on the family by his disobedience to parental authority.

The whole transaction shows up the indisputable fact that every sinner in all the world is simply a backslider, having by the wondeful redeeming grace of God in Christ being born a Christian. His *bona fide* citizenship in the Lord's kingdom all Bible teachers see abundantly demonstrated in His treatment of the babies everywhere, taking them into His arms, and certifying, "of such is my kingdom."

The Holy Ghost is the Executive of the trinity, the Convicter of the sinner, the Regenerater of the penitent, the Restorer of the backslider, the Sanctifier of the Christian, and the Glorifier of the pilgrims, when this mortal shall put on immortality. His contemptuous rejection, which is the meaning of "blasphemy" (Matt. 12:21-22), is in its nature an unpardonable sin. Heaven's bank has three officers, the Father, President; Son, Cashier; and the Holy Ghost, Teller, while the Bible is our checkbook, crowded full from lid to lid. We present all our checks to the Cashier. He turns them over to the Teller, who handles all the money, and never fails to hand out the gold of Ophir in so copious effusion as to make your head swin. At the same time He responds with a smile, "Why did you not check for more, as we have plenty and the larger the draft the more you honor the bank, which is absolutely unbankruptible."

We must remember that we can only receive at the Teller window, and consequently "No" to the Holy Ghost means damnation. "There is a time, we know not when, a point, we know not where, which marks the destiny of men to glory or despair. There is a time, by us unseen, which crosses every path, the hidden boundary between God's mercy and His wrath." We may sin away the day of grace and cross the fatal line, like the antediluvians, like Pharaoh and his magnates, and the Jewish church, who rejected Jesus and crucified Him, and went down in their awful tribulation. The unsavables of the great Gentile dispensation, are destined soon to go down in the bloody Armageddon all because they grieved away the Holy Spirit and would not let God save them.

Jesus says in His valedictory sermon preached on Mount Olivet Wednesday before His crucifixion the following Friday that our tribulation will be shortened for the sake of the elect, *i. e.*, the many people who will be saved when the millennium ushers in. Daniel 12:12 certifies: "Blessed is he that cometh to the end of the 1,335 days," which will bring them to the millennium, otherwise He would not call them blessed.

John abundantly corroborates Daniel (Rev., 19) when he closes the chapter with these words: "The rest were slain by the sword proceeding out of the mouth of Him that sitteth on the horse," *i. e.*, the Lord Jesus Christ. Here we have Him in the capacity of a military chieftain leading His army on the last battlefield of the Armageddon, when all the kings go down in blood to rise no more. An angel stands on the sun, a covenient place to reach all the world, thus showing up the universality of this final conflict, and calling all the carnivorous beasts and birds to the royal banquet, that they may feast on the flesh of kings, and their grand army slain on the battlefield.

This is followed by the arrest of the Pope and Mohammed, and their final and hopeless ejectment into the lake of fire in outer darkness. Old King Diabolus, is then and there arrested by the apocolyptic angel (Michael, I trow), and locked up a prisoner in hell till the millennium thousand years have come and gone.

To be slain by the word of the Lord can have no meaning, but for the sin personality in the human heart to be destroyed, and for that soul saved from top to toe, shine and shout forever. The same consolatory truth is revealed (Acts, 15 ch.), where we see that all the people who survive the tribulation will be saved in the millennium. Hear the word of the Prophet Amos: "After these things I will return and build again the throne of David, which had fallen down, build again the ruins of the same and set it up, that the remainder of the peoples may seek out the Lord, even all those on whom His name has been called."

This council, consisting of apostles, elders, and brethren, is really the highest authority on this side of heaven, James, the Lord's brother, presiding over it; Peter, the senior apostle, delivering the speech which focalized their verdict. Paul, the author of Acts, and Luke, the writer, Amos and Moses both quoted, thus giving us the *ipse dixit* of six inspired apostles and prophets certifying that all the people who survive the great and awful tribulation destined soon to come on the earth will be saved on the oncoming millennium. No wonder, because there will be no Devil here to humbug them with the beautiful speeches of his false prophet, who now hoax the millions, to run after priestcraft, churchism, legalism, and multitudism, Satanic inventions for the delusion and damnation of the multitudes he is driving like cattle down the broad road to fill up hell while he has an opportunity. Misery loves company and the people debauched, sidetracked and hopelessly ruined, are doing their utmost to engulf all others in the rayless midnight of a bottomless hell.

The Holy Spirit is the author of the Bible, our guide book, from a ruined world, up to bright celestial glory. He executes His mighty works through the media of the nine graces, by which we are saved (Eph. 5:19), love, joy, peace, long-suffering, kindness, goodness, faith, meekness, and holiness. The Bible teaches us, Rom. 13:10: "Love is the fulfilling of the law." The conclusion follows that all of these are simply diversified phases of love. They all resolve into love (not *philia,* human love, but *agapee,* divine love), which is not anything else than the divine nature, John 4:8, 16, "God is love."

Therefore, joy is love exultant, leaping and shouting, with angelic rhapsody. Peace is love resting sweetly and deliciously in the arms of Jesus, saved by His grace and filled by His spirit; like the tired baby, perfectly satisfied and delectably resting in its mother's arms. Long-suffering is love at the burning stake, or lions' mouth, electrified by a vision of angels hovering all ready descended with a fiery chariot, to bear away the disembodied spirits to the home of the weary, tempest-tossed pilgrim. Gentleness is the sweet divine love, poured out in the heart by the Holy Ghost in regeneration (Rom. 5:5), and made perfect when Jesus baptizes with the Holy Ghost and fire, giving you a clean heart. He makes your love perfect, the Holy Spirit coming in to abide forever, thus making you a tip-top model gentleman or a paragon body, not to be discounted even in the society of angels.

Goodness is the love of God, metamorphosed into an angel of mercy, going everywhere, hunting an opportunity to do good; finding nothing too hard or obnoxious from a human standpoint. It is delighted to do anything, however menial and servile for the glory of God.

Meekness is love sitting down on the fertile soil of the very bottom of the valley of humiliation amid blooming flowers, delicious fruits, and genial breezes, with no liability to fall, as there is no lower place into which to tumble. Faith is love on the battle-field, pressing the war to the very gates of the enemy, every moment ready at the drum tap to rush to the thickest of the fight and the hottest of the battle; shouting the victory night and day. 1 John 5:4: "This is the victory that overcometh the world, even our faith."

"Temperance," E. V., is entirely too weak to translate the word here used by the Holy Spirit, *egkratia,* from *egoo, el* and *kratos,* government; consequently signifying that beautiful self-government perfectly harmonical with the law of God; utterly delighted to do His will on earth as the angels in heaven. Of course, it includes the exterminating war with the whisky devil and every other.

While we are all saved by the nine graces, which are imparted in regeneration and made perfect in sanctification, we save others by the nine gifts which constitute our panoply (1 Cor. 12:8, 11), wisdom, knowledge, faith, bodily healing, manipulations of dynamites, prophecy, discernment of spirits, tongues and the interpretation of tongues, all these are given by one and the same Spirit. He dispenses to each one as He willeth, hence you see that the Holy Spirit is the custodian of the gifts. He is an armor-bearer and carries our panoply, so we will be disencumbered in the fight, ready to leap over a wall or run through a troop, thus elastic and light as a bird of paradise.

We see this beautifully illustrated soon after Saul was anointed king of Israel, because the Philistines, a nation of giants on the border, were whipping them so badly, having actually cut the peninsular in twain. This is what Sherman did to the Confederacy when he cut his way through from Atlanta to the sea, thus breaking the power and blighting the hope of Dixie Land ever gaining their independence, as the East and the West could no longer co-operate. So the Philistines had cut the peninsular of Palestine in twain and captured Micmash, a strong citadel on Jordan's banks. At midnight Jonathan, with a lonely armor-bearer managed to enter the citadel. They climbed the tower and shouted the victory, God sending a panic through the whole army superinducing a universal stampede. They thought Saul and his embattled hosts were on them. The Israelites did rally when they heard the shout of victory by Jonathan and his armor-bearer. They headed off the stampede, slaying them in piles, heaping the earth with mountains of the dead. Thus they achieved a grand and decisive victory over their formidable enemies, who so long had been to them a perpetual eye-sore.

This beautifully illustrates the consolatory fact that the Holy Ghost serves us as armor-bearer when we go out to fight the devil. He carries all of these important weapons, and imparts to us the very one we need in every part of the conflict with the world, the flesh and the devil. He leaves us all the time unencumbered to leap like an antelope, dash through the thickest brigade, hewing our way to the wall and jumping over it.

Here we see the mistake of the tongue people. The gift of tongues as a blessing is a trick of the devil to cheat you out of your sanctification, so he will get you in the end. We must watch. I was born and reared in the wild mountains abounding in game. Out at my work in the woods, my dog smelling all around, ran on a wild hen with her chickens. She takes to wing at once, in order to decoy the dog away from her chickens, and I see her flying and my dog after her like he was shot out of a cannon. Anon he touches the tip of her tail with his nose when she speeds off, as her wings are faster than her feet, and fearing that he may give her up and stop her pursuit, she drops down on the ground, taking it pedestrian till the dog is just about to take her in his mouth. He is running himself almost to death to get her, when thinking she has put distance enough between him and her panic-stricken chicks hidden in the leaves, she suddenly flies up in a tree. The dog looks up and tries to bark, but faint with fatigue, gives up in despair and comes away to me. She sits and takes a much-needed rest, till she sees our eyes turned away, when she flies back to the scene of conflict, clucks up her chickens and counts them, to her infinite joy, finding all there.

In a similar manner Satan utilizes all of his three blessings, simply to cheat you out of your sanctification, without which no one shall see the Lord. Heb. 12:14.

The tongue people claim that gift as a third blessing. They are mistaken, because we see (1 Cor., 13th ch.) Paul says: "Though I speak with tongues of men and of angels, *i. e.*, all the language spoken by all the people in the world and the angels in heaven and have not love, *i. e.*, (*agapee*, which is the divine nature, 1 John 4:8, 19, and we receive it in regeneration and it is made perfect in sanctification). "I am a sounding brass and a tinkling symbol," *i. e.*, I have nothing and am lost forever. We are not saved by the gifts, but the graces, and use the gifts to save others, as they constitute an armor. The false prophet Balaam had the gift of prophecy, and God through him gave us some beautiful Scriptures. Caiaphas, the wicked high priest who led the mob to murder Jesus, God used to give us the prophecy, John 11: "It is better that one die for the people than that they all die."

The donkey which Balaam rode had the gift of tongues, and spoke to him in human language, though he had no soul to save. Hence we see the foolishness of saying that the gift of tongues is essential to salvation. In this chapter Paul refers to the perfection of glory which we will all receive when this mortal puts on immortality. "When that which is perfect is come, that which is in part shall be done away. Whether there be prophesies, they shall fail, or knowledge, it shall be done away, or tongues, they shall cease."

Here we see the glorious triumph of the Christian soldier when he has fought his last battle and lays his armor down and flies away to the mount of victory, with angelic velocity. He never again will see an enemy, and consequently it would be exceedingly impertinent to encumber him with the panoply. What would you think of a Christian soldier walking over the field of glory a million years with a musket on his shoulder looking for a devil that he may shoot when he will never see one in all the flight of eternal ages!

You would say: "Brother, put away your gun and go to shouting, as you will never have any more use for it." Hence, we see the tongue people are farther from the truth than any of their predecessors on this diabolical three blessing line. First, "The Power," Acts 1:8: "You shall receive power after the Holy Ghost has come upon you," a wrong translation. It should read, "You shall receive the power of the Holy Ghost having come on you." Showing that the Holy Spirit is the only Power and if you seek anything else you are sidetracked by the devil to cheat you out of your sanctification, as he well knows in that case he will get you.

The second Satanic departure after the three blessings was that of fire, Matt. 3:11: "He will baptize you with the Holy Ghost and with fire, especially emphasizing the preposition "with," which is not in the original. It simply reads, "He will baptize you with the Holy Ghost and fire." The same apostle (Eph. 4:5) certifies there is but one baptism which Jesus gives, and without which your soul is forever lost. The ordinance with water is no baptism at all, but simply the outward sign.

This exposes the foolish heresy of baptismal regeneration preached by Catholics, Campbellites and Mormons, humbugging the people with the vain delusion that they are Christians, when they are only converts to the above heresies. Jesus says, Matt.,

23d ch.: "Twofold more the children of hell than before they joined the heretical churches."

We see to our sorrow in the tongue movement so many dear Holiness people, diabolically robbed of their experience, having the demoniacal gibberish, but no experience. They grieved away the Holy Ghost by tinkering with the demons, who are so dangerous because they are all fallen angels, older than Adam would be if still living on the earth. They have had so long a time to learn, whereas they were wiser and stronger than any of us at the beginning. The serious trouble is that they are determined to never let go till they drag their deluded victims into hell.

Of these nine gifts constituting the panoply of the Christian soldier, you see wisdom stands at the head of the catalogue, which means the right use of knowledge. My maternal ancestors, O'Kelley in Ireland and Kelley in America, migrated into Kentucky when it was a howling wilderness, inhabited by wild beasts and savages. They built their round log, clapboard-roof, and puncheon-floor cabin in the wild woods. Squatters lived about here and there, clearing up the ground and plowing the rich, virgin soil. Ere long the baby died, after winning the love of all the family by its beauty and innocence. As there was no priest to baptize it, they all wept and wailed over its mournful fate in the fires of purgatory; and put out runners in all directions hunting a Catholic priest to pray it out of the purgatorial fires. They signally failed, because none of them had at that time crossed the stormy ocean to look after their people, immigrated from the Old to the New World. Running on a squatter who was very ignorant, he

said to them, "I am acquainted with this entire settlement and assure you that there is no Catholic
priest; but there is a man going around, called a circuit rider, and I would not be surprised if he is the
very man you want." It so happened in the providence of God Bishop Asbury, from the Baltimore
Conference, had sent James Hall, the first Methodist
preacher west of the Allegheny Mountains, giving
him all of Kentucky for his circuit. At that time he
happened to be in the neighborhood, faithful on his
rounds, preaching every day in the cabins or under
the gum trees. They said to him: "Do send him to
us at once, as we are in dire trouble, thinking constantly about the sweet baby in the fires of purgatory. Fortunately, the squatter met him, delivered
his message, and gave him directions to the Irish
cabin.

He goes at once, dismounts and knocks at the
door, which promptly opens and he salutes the in-
mates. "I am the circuit rider for whom you sent."
They responded, "O! we want a priest to get the
dear baby out of purgatory. Are you a priest?"
Now comes in wisdom, as he would have lost the job
if he had said no, but as he had the gift of wisdom
conferred by the Holy Spirit he said, "Yes." (Which
was true, because every called and sent preacher of
the Gospel is a priest.) Then they said, as they
wanted to make sure, "Are you a Roman Catholic
priest?" Of course, he could not say yes, and if he
said no, he would lose his job, which he must hold
for the glory of God. He gave them an indirect
answer, "Not exactly, but I can do anything and
everything that a Roman Catholic priest can do."
His answer wonderfully encouraged them. As none

of them could read, they were superstitious, Catholics believing that the priest had power to remit sins and get souls out of purgatory. Then they said, "Do, please, get the baby out of purgatory."

When he responded, "I have already had the case before God and am happy to say to you that the baby is not in purgatory, but in heaven, and the prettiest thing you ever saw. The angels all want it in their arms at the same time." This pleased them so that they almost died of joy and said, "Holy father, do please come and see us whenever you can." Here you see the gift of wisdom again; as he had no church edifice and he did all of his preaching in the homes of the squatters, he said: "One month from this day, at this hour, look for me and tell all your friends to come."

He published it everywhere he went, and when the day rolled around, even before the hour, the cabin was overcrowded with the red-hot Methodists. (For the devil had not yet invented the Methodist ice factory which is now doing a land office business for the population of hell.) O! how they make the forest roar with their full salvation songs, their fire-baptized prayers, and roaring shouts, till it seemed that every clapboard will leave the roof and fly to the stars, and their rousing jumps will surely break through the puncheon floor. The result is that all the family with others, not a few, fall on the floor and cry aloud for mercy till they pray them through. The preacher takes them all into the Methodist Church, and whence they have gone to the ends of the earth preaching the everlasting Gospel with the Holy Ghost sent down from heaven. Your humble servant has the honor to be "one of them," having preached sixty-six years, around the historic world four times and through the great heathen fields, India, Burma, Malaysia, China, Japan, and Africa, and I am the author of 222 books on Bible Holiness, every one telling the sure way to heaven.

Hence, you see the infinite value of these spiritual gifts, so efficiently utilized by the Holy Ghost, through the humble instrumentality of the first Methodist preacher ever in Kentucky, a woodsman who had never rubbed against a college.

The second gift is knowledge, which means the supernatural insight into the divine truth which the Holy Ghost alone can give, to the humble, faithful student of His precious Word. We are all saved by it, sanctified, fortified, fed, and will be glorified when this mortal puts on immortality.

The third gift is faith; not the grace of faith by which we are saved, but the gift of faith by which we save others. Therefore, be sure that you go to God and seek until you hear from heaven for every soul laid on your heart in prayer. A woman in Indiana whose husband was a wild steamboat captain, running from Cairo, Ill., to New Orleans, La., was gloriously sanctified. She plead with God for her noble husband, the father of her children, till he answered her at midnight, "You have him." The next morning a boy brings a telegram which she reads, stating that her husband's boat is burned and he with it.

She reads it, folded it up, hands it back to the boy with orders to take it to the office and "tell the operator that it is a mistake; my husband is coming home to get religion and go with me to heaven." When the operator read it he said to the bystanders, "Look after that poor woman at once, as you see she has gone crazy, the awful news having utterly upset her mind." Three days rolled away and he came home. She met him at the door and told him of her prevailing prayer, when she heard from heaven that he was coming home and get religion and go with her to glory. This time a thunderbolt leaped from heaven through his heart and he fell sprawling on the floor, roaring aloud. She sent her children in all directions to call in the Holiness people, who prayed for him all night and with the breaking day the glorious Son of Brightness rose on him with healing in His wings, sweeping him into the kingdom. Pressing on to sanctification, he takes his stand beside his noble better half in the leadership of the Holiness army in lovely Hoosier land.

The fourth gift is Divine Healing, which you need for your own health to prolong life that you may not verify the Bible verdict. "The wicked shall not live out half their days." Tobacco and all alcoholic drinks as well as opium are narcotic poisons, sure to kill sooner or later, while coffee and tea have no nutriment. They simply operate like the whip and spur on the horse, stirring him up to greater speed, and wearing him out the sooner. It makes you prematurely old, so you die before your time, and seriously cut down your reward in heaven. As God made the body, He alone can repair it; the greatest physicians in the world whom I have consulted in my journey all the way around the world positively say that they have no power to heal diseases, but only to assist nature in the capacity of a good nurse. They are useful mechanically to set broken bones and perform surgical operations; diag-

nostically, to tell what the disease is, and hygienic-
ally, to tell us how to live in harmony with the laws
of nature.

The Great Physician heals disease all the time
which the doctors have utterly given up. If you
have it not, send for my book on Divine Healing,
only 10 cents. It is in my library of eighty-eight,
everyone on a different subject, and telling you the
sure way to heaven, selling for a dime per copy, *i. e.*,
$8.00, and get it from me for only $3.00, an effort
of mine to spread Scriptural Holiness over the earth.
You can read them all and then sell them out for
more than double the cost; at the same time doing
good which you will only know in eternity.

Only a few days ago a sister wrote me from De-
troit, Mich., stating she had a sore on her body for
thirty-six years, and it was growing constantly, and
by all the doctors pronounced incurable. I had the
school pray for her healing and wrote to her how to
get it by turning over her body to God forever for
a temple of the Holy Ghost, to be used only in the
interest of His kingdom, and receiving healing by
simple faith, believing that He does heal, and so
abiding in the perpetual exercise of faith for healing that He does heal now. After six weeks she
wrote me, stating she had followed my directions
and that it was actually getting well.

The fifth gift working miracles, *energemata
dunameites*, manipulations of dynamites. Dynamite
is God's only definition of Gospel, Rom. 1:16. The
Gospel is the dynamite of God unto salvation to
everyone that believes. The reason why we need
all the Holiness people for preachers is because they

are the only people in the world who preach the Gospel.

N. B.—Dynamite is the greatest explosive in the world, therefore, the Gospel is that mysterious spirituality which blows the devil out of the sinner and depravity, *i. e.*, the devil nature, *i. e.*, inbred sin out of the Christian. The popular gospel, human eloquence without a scintilla of dynamite, is the devil's greased plank over which he is sliding the millions of the popular churches into hell. You know that the popular gospel is destitute of dynamite, which illustrates the sad fact that it is not akin to the Gospel of the Lord Jesus Christ, which blows up the devil kingdom every time, stirs hell and makes Satan rage, but it is Satan's counterfeit for the delusion and damnation of souls.

The next gift is prophecy, pronounced by Paul (1 Cor., 14th ch.) the most important of the nine. It means preaching, which is God's method of saving the world, and we in His infallible wisdom are honored above the angels with the investiture of their wonderful commission, in these earthen vessels to carry the message of salvation to the ends of the earth. V. 3 gives us God's definition of preaching. Look at it and say "yes" with an emphasis that will make devils howl and angels shout. "He that prophesieth speaketh unto the people edification, exhortation and comfort." Hence, you see you are to give everybody you meet a sermon, consisting of three divisions. First, with the candor of the judgment bar, tell what he is, where he is, and whither he is going. Secondly, exhort him with a brilliant picture of a bottomless hell, a topless heaven, and a boundless eternity. Finally give the wonderful prom-

ises of God ringing the heavenly bells through the
Bible from Alpha to Omega every man, woman, and
child who has the experience of salvation in the
heart is competent by the Holy Spirit always freely
given to preach the Gospel to every immortal soul
you meet in your pilgrimage. Thus we heroically
verify our Savior's commandment, "Lay not up for
yourselves treasures upon earth, where moth and
rust corrupt, and thieves break through and steal.
But lay up treasures in heaven where neither moth
nor rust corrupt, nor thieves break through and
steal. For where your treasure is there will your
heart be also."

The seventh gift is discernment of spirits, which
you need in order to utilize the Lord's ammunition
and not waste it on dead game. Heed the warning
of Jesus, "Cast not your pearls before swine, lest
they trample them under their feet, turn again and
eat you up; nor give that which is holy to the dogs."
This means that you are not to preach sanctification to sinners, dead professors, backsliders, and
hypocrites, but, like John the Baptist and Jesus,
"Repent, for the kingdom of heaven is at hand."

Early in the Holiness Movement in Dixie Land
I went to a camp-meeting in East Tennessee. I
found a great multitude listening spellbound to a
great Holiness evangelist preaching sanctification.
When he wound up with an altar call very few responded, and they from a distance. He asked me to
speak. Looking around, the Lord at once brilliantly
flooded me with this gift, so I read the people like
I read the Greek and I proceeded to observe, "I am
not going to preach sanctification to you people, as
it is only for those who have been truly born from

above. You must receive the supernatural birth, witnessed by the Holy Spirit, before you can possibly seek and find the sanctification without which no one shall see the Lord. The other evangelist soon left, turning over the laboring oar to your humble servant, who took his stand on Mount Sinai, crying to God from the depths of his soul to furnish the thunderbolt, lightning shafts and earthquakes, which he tossed from the tips of his fingers.

At that day the opposition was terrific, the evil reports going before us, and stirring up the carnal rabble, worldly churches, and anti-Holiness preachers against us. In this case a few people who believed in Holiness had brought the camp thither that the people might be saved and sanctified. The multitude in the churches and outside were awfully prejudiced against us, so that the Methodist pastor wrote me a letter, ordering me to leave, or he would prosecute me as an invader. I wrote on the blank page of his letter a loving invitation to come along to meeting and let us pray together that God may drop down from heaven the much-needed revival.

We moved on until Sunday, when the crowd was immense all day. I still stood on Mount Sinai, preaching the Gospel of conviction, the horrors of hell, and the doom of the damned with all my might; feeling all day that a cyclone had left heaven and was moving towards us. In the evening service during the introductory, I realized that the cyclone was near, and when I got up to preach the moment I announced my text it struck the camp. The multitudes of sinners, backsliders, dead professors, and hypocrites, uninvited rushed to the altar from all parts of the large tabernacle, filling it to overflowing and the aisles all around.

At the same time the Holiness band from Knoxville, who had come out to work in the meeting, received the wonderful gift of the spirit and broke out preaching on all sides. The altar service beginning at that early hour moved like a hurricane till way past midnight and into the morning hours. People triumphant passed from death unto the life, and through the flooded Jordan into Beulahland, with tremendous shouts of victory. You need this gift in all your soul-saving work, to fortify you against dangers of wasting your ammunition.

The eighth gift is tongues, which simply means language, and you must have it; cannot do without it. The English language contains 458,000 words, of which the common people only use three or four hundred. Great scholars but eight or ten thousand. Hence, you see the grand scope for the gift of the English language. So you will never run out of words. Before the Lord sanctified me forty-nine years ago, I was a college graduate, and working hard, made my sermon by the power of my intellect and education. I did not know how to preach with the Holy Ghost sent down from heaven. By hard work I made a vast diversity of sermons; but when the Lord gave me that wonderful fire baptism it burned up the Mason, the Odd Fellow, the college president, and the Southern Methodist preacher. It left only John the Baptist now, who ignored his personality, saying that he was only a voice telling them the word of God. The same fire burned up all of my sermons, and the blessed Holy Spirit filling my

4

soul, imparted to me His gifts, that of tongues, among the other eight, actually making me a preaching machine, so I am always ready, and the more I say the more I have on hand.

If you go to the foreign field, rest assured the Holy Ghost will give you their language, as He did at Pentecost; though not superseding your own efforts to learn it, as He sets no premium on laziness.

The last gift is interpretation, which you so much need to qualify you to learn the beautiful Greek into which the New Testament was written; and wonderful Hebrew which God gave Adam and Eve and is doubtless now spoken in heaven. These languages are so necessary to understand the Lord's precious Word and really known by the Holy Spirit alone, who will lovingly give them to you, delightfully co-operating with your own efforts. He makes the language easy, thrilling, interesting, and transcendingly edifying.

You need this gift to qualify you to understand the grand old English Bible, and the beautiful Holiness literature which now in His good providence inundates Christendom. Amid all your study of languages beware of the tongue heresy which is no language, and consequently no tongue, and never has been. Satan couterfeits everything God does. He cannot give you a language, but can give you noises like birds and frogs as his preachers, wizards, witches, sorcerers, necromancers, jugglers, Mormons and Spiritualists in all ages. Isaiah 8:19, "Wizards that peep and mutter." When I was preaching to the heathen ten years ago the devil worshippers in India had this same counterfeit tongue.

CHAPTER III

HAMITH HAPPEKETH

This Hebrew word (Gen. 3:24) is translated turning every way and has the striking peculiarity of automatism, *i. e.*, self-activity, in that grand old language which God gave Adam and Eve and is no doubt now the popular dialect of heaven, is known in Hebrew grammar as Hithpael.

The Australian boomerang is thrown at a person with the intention of killing him, because it fastens on him and sticks to him till it executes its fatal work. If the thrower is unskillful, it turns back, fastens on him and kills him. Consequently it is a very dangerous experiment, as when thrown it is sure to kill somebody. This illustrates the wonderful word of God, which means death all the time. It is heaven's waybill, the question is settled forever, that the King's highway is a death route all the time. Really it is Satan's counterfeit, if it does not kill the old man of sin.

You may handle the word of God deceitfully and the old man flourishes like a green bay tree, spreading its branches till he repines for hell fire. But if you read it with a sincere and honest mind, it will always verify the Australian boomerang. Mark its thread with the blood of Calvary, which means the death of sin and the life of Christ.

Two English noblemen, Lord Littleton, and Boling Broke, both honest infidels, disciples of Tom Payne, were conversing together about the Bible. They mutually agreed to write a refutation of it,

showing it up false and mythical. The one chose
for his subject the resurrection of Christ, and the
other the conversion of Saul of Tarsus. Both did
their work and met again, to their mutual surprise.
Each dreaded to meet the other, because he had been
converted. Both divulged the good news, they
shouted together in the kingdom of God, and going
out proclaimed the glad tidings of this wonderful
salvation.

During the Revolutionary War two young men,
Stith Meade, and his comrade, both sons of Methodist parents, were traveling horseback through the
Carolinas and ran out of money. Of course, they
had to stop and work or beg their way. Too proud
for the latter, they mutually agreed to play preachers. About 4 o'clock in the afternoon they inquired
for Methodists living on the road, and learned the
name of an old class teacher, whose house they would
reach about nightfall.

Riding up to the gate, they called, and he came
out, and they asked him if he entertained Methodist
preachers, and he shouted, "O, yes, so glad you have
come! Dismount and be at home." Turning around
he roared aloud to his boys, giving everyone of them
the route to run in every direction to tell all the
members of his class and everybody else that two
Methodist preachers had stopped at his house, and
for all to come to the meeting. Of course, that was
to those wicked youths a thunderbolt from a cloud-
less sky. They had no dream of having their false
profession put to the test. Of course, they walked
in courteously, preacher-like, receiving introduction
to the family and saluting them accordingly. Now
they asked to be excused and all set to their work

to entertain them and get ready for the meeting. As soon as their attention was turned away they walked out and consulted together, "What are we to do, as we are going to have a congregation expecting us to preach to them when we are utterly incompetent, and not preachers at all, but lying tramps!"

The case was awful and their embarrassment serious in the extreme. Stith then said that he thought he could make a pretty good stagger at some of his father's old sermons, which he had heard so often that he knew them by heart, and he would do the preaching the best he could, if his comrade would do the singing and praying. He conveniently dodged through by just letting the old class leader attend to it, who with his fire-baptised members was in all his glory and moved it off with a revival swing. The congregation continued to gather from all directions till the house run over and the time arrived for preaching, all looking at the new preacher and expecting a royal banquet.

Stith was in an awful dilemma, as he had to preach to the crowded house, so many of them brilliant saints and good judges of preaching, when he was nothing but a sinner. Of course, he was inwardly crying to God to have mercy and help him in his awful undertaking to preach to the people the salvation he did not possess himself. He had inherited preaching gifts from his father, and was really called to preach, though yet a sinner.

He moved off the best he could, and as he said afterwards, he found it the hardest job he had ever tried in his life the first ten minutes. Then he forgot himself, no longer recognizing his environment, until he found himself at midnight with a glorious shout with many others. Thus he had actually been gloriously converted while preaching, and got so happy that he preached about two hours. He invited mourners. Many came, prayed through, shouted the victory, and among them his traveling companion (whose name has slipped my memory), who was gloriously converted. Decidedly, the Devil overshot himself, thinking to hurt the cause of God by having these young men lie and cheat their passage, when he lost both of them, as Stith Meade became a great preacher in his generation, and the other one a grand success in the ministry of the gospel.

This illustrates the automatism of God's word. My amanuensis asked me what automatism means. It is from the Greek *Autos,* which means itself, and we say a perpetual motion, like a watch that runs forever, without winding. Really, it is a machine which all ages have been trying in vain to invent, and doubtless will never succeed, as God alone is perfectly omnipotent, omnipresent and omniscient within Himself. Everything else in the boundless universe depends on Him. Here we see their word, which is the subject of the chapter, shows that God's truth has its own power in it and if infidels and skeptics are only honest, they will all get converted and saved simply by reading it.

Saul of Tarsus believed Jesus was an impostor, and deserved the crucifixion He had received till God gave him a look on Him. This practically revolutionized him, so he turned at once a complete somersault, thus from top to toe metamorphosed, so the astonishing news went on the wings of the wind to the ends of the earth, "He who once persecuted

us now preaches the faith, which he then destroyed."
He moved in a cyclone of fire, till he lost his head on
Nero's block and flew away to glory to meet the
glorified Christ he had so heroically preached.

The Lord used my humble instrumentality to pioneer the holiness movement from the Atlantic to the
Pacific.   When we launched the work in Denver,
Col., we met violent opposition, as everywhere else.
Charley Allen, a brilliant young Methodist preacher,
got wonderfully sanctified, and so much dreaded to
meet his Presiding Elder, who was fighting the movement with all his might.   But of course he was
obliged to meet him very soon, and Oh, how surprised to find him deeply converted and anxious to
meet Charley that he might tell him how to get it and
pray for him.   God had used the very report of
Charley's experience to convict the Presiding Elder.
He gladly crossed the Jordan and met the young
preacher in the happy land of Canaan, where milk
and honey flow, corn and wine abound, flowers never
fade, and fruits never fail; winter never comes and
summer ever lasts.

"Holiness or Hell" was one of the first books of
my writing among my two hundred and twenty-two
on Bible holiness.   The very name produced a sen-
sation among the holiness fighters.   A Methodist
bishop actually carried it with him to his conferences, held it up before his preachers and abused it,
stating that it was a shame that a Methodist
preacher ever wrote such a book.   Thus he gave it
the grandest advertisement, though inadvertantly.
I could not have it made fast enough to meet the
demand, as everyone that heard him said, "I must
have that book and see what is in it."   An anti-

holiness pastor in Colorado actually got convicted
for sanctification just by looking at the title before
he ever read the book, and called me to his work to
preach it to his people.

There is an unseen power in God's word, which
will paddle its own canoe if you only let it have a
chance. In our Savior's Sermon on the Mount, He
gives us a Judgment scene, preachers crying out,
"Have we not prophesied in Thy name and in Thy
name cast out demons, and in Thy name done many
wonderful works?" Then will I confess unto them
"I never knew you; depart from me, ye workers of
iniquity." You see, demons had been cast out, souls
saved under their ministry, though themselves forever lost. Remember, the truth of God does the
saving, even though preached by the devil, or a sinner who is an incarnate demon.

John A. Murrell, the notorious Tennessee robber,
was a powerful preacher, sending out appointments
in advance of his gang. Always he ascertained the
leading denomination and announced himself as a
preacher in that church. Under his powerful preaching he got them down on their knees, while his men
would be out stealing their horses. The moment the
word reached the audience he mounts a bench and
roars aloud, "Brethren, you must look after your
stock as the thieves are about. In the pell-mell
skedaddle he slipped away, joining his gang and
going on their way, the terror of the pioneers.

It is indispensable that we have God's preachers,
and lamentable to have the Devil's, not only highway
robbers, thieves and murderers, but high-toned gen-
tlemen, with fine educations, yet not knowing the
Lord. We must remember that every tub stands on

its own bottom, and God's word, "Seek and ye shall find, ask and ye shall receive, knock and it shall be opened unto you. In the day thou seekest Me with thy whole heart I will be found of thee," is perfectly true, and God will always honor it, even though preached by the vilest sinner. Hence the infinite value of God's word, which we should all do our utmost to dispense to the ends of the earth, as it is always and everywhere the power of God unto salvation to everyone that believeth.

In 1800 and 1801 the pioneers had a camp meeting at Cane Ridge, Kentucky, pitched for ten days. But it was attended with so paradoxical results that it ran on all summer and fall till winter storms and deep snow alone could break it up. The people hearing, had come from far and near, crowding the brush arbor till it was actually eclipsed by the thronging multitudes filling the wood in all directions.

James B. Finley, living up in Ohio, heard of the wonderful scenes there transpiring; the people falling and lying prostrate, jerking as if they would break to pieces, the women's long hair disheveled, streaming down, and cracking like whip lashes, under all sorts of contortions. This young man boasted himself the champion of the age, and as he was an infidel, he swore that they could not knock him down. He mounted his horse, as there were no public conveyances, and rode all the way.

On his arrival he finds a great multitude under the majestic forest trees, and about twenty preachers scattered about everywhere, standing in wagons, or on stumps, or logs, or rocks, and all preaching with a vehemence he had never seen before. He hitched his horse and came into the crowd, congratulating

himself proof against the knock-down power which
he saw on all sides. People were falling, rolling on
the ground, leaping and jerking.

He had not been there long till a strange weakness comes into his body, and he finds himself about
to fall. He even finds it necessary to get away in
order to keep from falling. But, behold, that weakness continues! He bolsters up his championship,
the boasted bully of the age, and says to himself,
"I have ridden my horse one hundred miles to show
the people that there is one man that can stand anything these fanatics can do and they cannot knock
me down." Again that unaccountable weakness
comes on him, so he hastens away to keep from falling. This time he mounts his horse, and riding to
a store buys some brandy and returns with Napo-
leonic determination, "I will have the victory over
all this strange influence coming over me."

Hitching his horse again, he goes to the edge of
the crowd, where he can hear the preaching. His
attention is attracted to a crowd of about five hundred, who had recently arrived. "I will look at them
and see how they stand it," he said, doing his utmost
by his will power to fortify himself against the
excitement, carrying the people on the wing of a
tornado. While looking at that crowd he sees them
all on the ground as if a battery of a thousand guns
had been turned on them simultaneously. Some
rolled and cried aloud, others leaped into the air,
and, O, the jerking, as if their bodies would break
to pieces.

Soon they began to rise and make the welkin roar
with tremendous shouts of victory, to Him who is
mighty to have, and strong to deliver. While con-

templating the scene, he finds himself actually falling, and hastened away, inwardly soliloquizing, "If I can only get away, I will go back home and never come again, as I see if I stay here I will be rolling, jumping, jerking, screaming and agonizing like the rest." Though active as a catamount, he found his body too weak and trembling to mount. He had to lead his horse up to a big log in order to get on him, and then hold to the saddle horn, and content himself to ride in a walk, in order to keep from falling off. He had traveled about ten miles with difficulty, sitting in the saddle, holding to the horn, and he was passing through a village when he actually fell off the horse, like a dying man. The people all stood aloof, afraid to go about him lest he had some contagious disease.

An old Dutchman, who had been to the camp, and had been knocked down, came to him, and said to the people, "Do not be afraid to minister to this man. There is nothing the matter with him but conviction for his sins. He has been to that wonderful camp-meeting." So with difficulty he prevailed on the people to help him carry him into the house. He and all the help he could get prayed for him all night, and with the morning dawn the glorious heavenly daybreak flooded his agonizing soul. His strength returned, so he mounted his horse, came home, told the thrilling news, corroborating everything they had heard in reference to the knock down power, jerks, convulsions, and contortions attending the miraculous convictions and sky blue conversions in that wonderful meeting. This young man became a Methodist preacher, and lived long to preach the Gospel in the pioneer settlements of this great country, at that time the rendezvous of multitudes from the old world.

The exegesis of this marvelous revival was the simple fact that the French infidels were at that time in the lead of that nation, and their books, and especially Payne's "Age of Reason" (which won so many disciples and among them Bob Ingersoll), were circulated throughout this new country, and were about to capture it for the devil. God looked down in mercy and answered this prayer of the pioneer saints, sending that knock down revival.

I have often seen the same power in my own meetings, twenty-five and forty-five years ago. The people fell under the power of the Holy Ghost in the morning meeting, and would lie prostrate and unable to stand on their feet, until the afternoon meeting. The power would come still stronger, and knock down a lot more, and as the mourners could not travel, we would stay with them until the night meeting. In the great crowd dozens, scores, and hundreds would fall, and all lie prostrate till the resurrection power created the new man in the heart, and raised them up to shout the victory. They roared like Gabriel's trumpet at all hours, day and night. We had no adjournment, for the good reason that so many of our congregation could not stand on their feet, till the Lord raised them up, which He always did in due time. These facts show up the miraculous power of the Gospel, which is the same yesterday, today and forever.

The life of James B. Finley was written, and if you could find it you would be much edified by reading it, and you would find the above sketch substantiated in his biography. Dr. Finney, of Oberlin,

Ohio (almost the same name), lived a generation subsequently and under his ministry, after the Lord so wonderfully sanctified him, he stirred the whole Anglo Saxon world. He crossed the ocean repeatedly, and preached to all nations, speaking the English language. In his ministry the power was so wonderfully manifested that the people fell whereever he went, whether in Europe or in America.

He walked into a cotton factory in New York, working seven hundred hands, and entering the loom room where the clatter of three hundred steam looms utterly disqualified them to hear his voice; he stood motionless as a statue and looked on them. When the girls got their eyes on him and his very pysiognomy, flashing the heavenly radiance like an angel's, so convicted them that they lost the thread and tried in vain to recover it. They got so tangled up that they sent for the boss, who came in to relieve the entanglement. The face and presence of the silent visitor sent a thrill to his heart which disqualified him to extricate the confusion. It so convicted him that he sent a runner to the engineer with orders to stop the engine, take off the power, and notify all the operators to come into the loom room. The preacher found himself surrounded by an audience of from 500 to 700 before he said a word. Quite a number of them had already fallen down on the floor, seeking the God who had sent His prophet into their midst. Thus he found a great revival on his hands, just dropped down from heaven before he spoke a word. The Holy Ghost had so efficiently pioneered the way that the man of God had this grand wide open door, and all of those people crying out like the Philipian jailor, "What shall I do to be saved?"

These wonderful demonstrations, gloriously confirm the only definition of the Gospel given in the Bible. Rom. 1:16, "The Gospel is the dynamite of God unto salvation to everyone that believeth."

During the Civil War Kentucky and Maryland stood by the Stars and Stripes, while all their sisters throughout Dixie Land, from the Atlantic to Mexico, followed the Stars and Bars into the Confederacy. The Dixie politicians rode all over Kentucky, speaking to spellbound multitudes to effect her secession from the Union, assuring us that if we would go out and present the North a solid South, there would be no war; and if they did try it a little that the Southern men were so brave that they would whip them twenty to one, and carry the war into the North where it belonged. They claimed that Northern politicians had brought it on by agitating against slavery.

When I was a little lad I read the Congressional news, stating that large sums of money were appropriated for the removal of Hellgate (certain formidable rocks in East River, Atlantic Ocean, between New York and Brooklyn, on which so many ships were wrecked), I said, "Amen," as I was a little Christian, and I thought it meant war against hell.

When the government built the great warships they drew so much water they could not pass those rocks, with all government effort to remove them it was not improved. When the Confederates opened the war by storming Fort Sumter, S. C., they advertised their campaign against New York City, which they could have taken, because the warships could not get into the harbor to protect her. Rather than have the Confederates bombard and burn her down they would have surrendered.

Consequently the city was in trepidation every hour, when a little man dropped down, diagnosed the situation, and said to the mayor and his magnates, "Give me money enough and I will take Hellgate out by the roots."

They responded, "Money is nothing if you can only do it."

Dynamite had just been discovered, and was unknown. He responded, "Rest easy, I will obligate myself in black and white, no cure, no pay."

So he entered upon the enterprise, sent men down under the sea in diving bells, to honeycomb the mountain, drilling holes all over it in which he deposited dynamite cartridges, so arranged as to be ignited by electricity.

He advertised in the papers the day at 10 A.M. when he would take Hellgate out by the roots. Never did New York know such a crowd; every street was packed and jammed, bridges and housetops were thronged. It gave rise to curiosity. He promised that his baby girl of three years should do that miraculous work. The hour had arrived, and a million eyes focalized on the spot in the blue sea where it was certified Hellgate stood.

The quietude is like a graveyard, all hearts beating with solicitude when the baby reaches her tiny finger and moved a wire six inches till it touched another and thus closes the circuit. With lightning velocity it transmitted electrical fire to all those dynamite cartridges. Suddenly there was a roar as if Vesuvius, Etna and Stromboli had all simultaneously exploded, shooting rivers of lava into the air. Instantaneously it lifted up the superencumbent sea, and deluging either shore, thus copiously baptizing the curious multitude. Before they can turn around falling back and splashing the sea dry, thus giving them the second baptism, when suddenly the elements are as silent as the graveyard. Hellgate was utterly blown out, with vast and valuable building stones and debris for street repairs. Now the greatest steamers in the world find unobstructed ingress and egress.

This is God's definition of Gochel, and the only one. Therefore where there is no dynamite to blow the devil out of sinners, and depravity out of Christians, there is no gospel. Reader, my prayer is that God may make you a dynamiter. Methinks you say "Amen, Load me up with dynamite and shoot me out at the devil." The mountains in the Bible give us a thrilling lesson, beginning with Sinai, where we have the dynamite of conviction, blowing out the Devil's rock, and bursting him up so he can neither eat nor sleep. I have been an indefatigable Sinai preacher, and never found a place too hard for me to have a glorious revival, if the people would only let me stay until I could drill and deposit the dynamite and shoot it off.

When I saw a nightmare of conviction settle down on the people, falling from their seats, crying for mercy as above portrayed, I left Sinai. I took my stand on Calvary, preaching the dying love of Jesus.

"In evil long I took delight,
　　Unawed by shame or fear,
Till a new object struck my sight,
　　And stopped my wild career!
I saw one hanging on a tree in agony and blood,
　　Who fixed His languid eyes on me,
As near the cross I stood.
　　My conscience felt and owned my guilt,
And plunged me in depsair;
　　I saw my sins His blood had spilt,
And helped to nail Him there.
　　A second look He gave,
Which said, "I freely all forgive,
　　My blood is for thy ransom paid,
I die that thou mayest live."

Thus I preached the Calvary Gospel till they believed it. The Holy Ghost through their faith imparts another dynamite blast, igniting it with a spark of heavenly fire. This blows you all the way out of the brick hills and mortar yard of Egyptian slavery, through the clefted sea to shout the victory. Fall into Miriam's triumphant procession, put on the panoply of the Egyptian army now at the bottom of the sea, and their arms floated ashore for your accommodation. You can join Joshua in his war with all those daring to obstruct your march for the happy land of Canaan.

I am eighty-four years old and was never attacked by a harlot but once in my life, though I have traveled more than any man you ever knew, four times around the historic world; crossing this continent immemorially. Walking in a dark place about mid-

night, waiting for a train at Newton, Kan., medi-
tating and praying as always, for the Lord has given
me 222 books in my travels, throughout the whole
world. In order to favor my weak eyes, I was walking to and fro and talking with the Lord. She suddenly came from behind a train, standing on the
track, and assaulted me with her libertinous solicita-
tions. Instead of running back into the depot, utterly ignoring her libertinous appeals, I did as I do
all people whom I meet in my travels, at once proceeded to preach the Gospel to her with all my might.
Like Paul on Areopagus, preaching to the Greek
philosophers, I did my very best for her soul, re-
maining utterly reticent on her diabolical line of
talk, in which she was so fluent, and at the same
time trying to pull me by the hand around behind
that train. But the longer she persisted, the more
indefatigably I preached the unsearchable riches of
Christ, with a gigantic hand shaking her over hell,
till she suddenly gave up her quest and fled away.

Therefore in all the assaults of Satan and his
myrmidons, we have nothing to do but walk in the
footprints of Jesus, who met the devil face to face
in the wilderness of Judea. First he tempted His
physical manhood to turn the stone into bread, and
thus satisfy His awful hunger, as He had eaten nothing in forty days. A single stroke with the sword
of the Spirit, utterly defeated the devil. Matt. 4:4,
"It is written man shall not live by bread alone, but
by every word that proceedeth out of the mouth of
God."

Then he leads Him forty miles to Jerusalem, into
the Temple and sits Him down on the highest pin-
nacle, tempting Him to jump, quoting Psa. 91, where

God had promised to have His angels guard Him so
He would never get hurt. Adroitly he left out
the clause, "in all Thy ways." This was a direct assault against His spiritual manhood, turning the
heaviest battering rams of the pandemonium against
His faith, which is the basal grace, in an attempt to
metamorphose it into presumption, the devil's counterfeit for faith. Again Jesus administers another
stroke with this wonderful flaming sword, God's
word. It is written, "Thou shalt not tempt the Lord
thy God."

Finally he leads Him across the valley of Jehosa-
phat, up to the summit of Mount Olivet, the highest
in all the Holy Land. In a panorama he shows Him
all the kingdoms of the world and the glory of the
same, and says "all this will I give unto thee, if thou
will fall down and worship me." Lucifer, the great
archangel, sinned in heaven, fell and was cast out
(Rev., 12th ch.) because he aspired to be a God instead of an archangel. He is still on that line,
adroitly playing God on the people. A thousand
million heathen worship the devil avowedly, in order
to appease his wrath and escape the punishment he
inflicts on all within the range of his possibility.
Three hundred million Mohammedans and 450,000,-
000 Catholics and not a few Protestants blindly and
unconsciously worship the devil now. They preach
a sinning religion. 1 John 3:8, "He that committeth
sin is of the devil," which sadly forces on us the conclusion that he has the big end of all the religions
in this world. None but the little sprinkle of Holiness people preach a religion that smashes up the
sinning business, saves to the uttermost and sanctifies wholly. They really preach the gospel of

Christ, which is the power of God unto salvation to everyone that believeth.

This time Jesus simply responded, it is written, "Thou shalt worship the Lord thy God and Him only shalt thou serve." Then Satan left Him from the simple fact that the American army retreated at the battle of Monmouth, because he had run out of ammunition and could do nothing else. In Satan's war against Adam the First, he conquered on his first round, captured Adam and Eve and everything they had, and is still on the throne of the world to-day, laying under contribution earth and hell to populate his kingdom while he can. He knows that his time is short when he will be driven from his kingdom, never to regain it in this world. In his battle with Adam the Second he used all his ammunition and lost it all. Christ did not need that victory, as He was infinitely glorious without it, but won it for you and me, and consequently we have nothing to do but tip our hats to the devil, be true to God and shout the victory forever.

Before the Methodist Church had a missionary society Bishop Soule rode his horse throughout the blue grass region of Kentucky, collecting money to support his missionaries whom he had sent into Jackson's Purchase, i. e., the land south of the Ohio River, east of the Mississippi River, west of the Tennessee River, and north of Tennessee, which the United States had bought from the French when Jackson was President. It was a howling wilderness, inhabited by wild beasts and savages; but after the purchase American squatters had poured in extensively, thus opening a wide door for missionaries. While the old Bishop was riding along through the dense, untrodden wilderness, a burly robber walked out, took his horse by the bridle, and ordered him to give up his money or die on the spot. He put his hand on his pocket and responded, "I tell you no lie, I have money, but it is God's and I am taking it to his poor missionaries and you cannot get it." Then he proceeded to preach the Gospel to him with the Holy Ghost from heaven. He turned pale, let go the bridle and disappeared in the thicket, while the man of God goes on his way rejoicing.

The last time I ever saw Bishop Kavanaugh, a native Kentuckian, we rode together on the train, after hearing me preach on sanctification the preceding night. It was before the movement had reached Dixie Land, and he entertained me delightfully telling about the pioneer Methodist Episcopal preachers of dear old Kentucky. He said: "John Sinclair, in his great woodland circuit, preaching every day in the cabins of the squatters had one unhewed log church. He was preaching on Sunday to a large audience, and three ruffians behaved so rudely that he reproved them severely, and they withdrew from the house and came back no more. Going ahead with the service and winding up with a class meeting, as they always did, the Lord sent down on them a sweeping landslide from heaven, bearing everything before it, and making the surrounding forest roar and reverberate with shouts of victory.

After adjournment, mounting his horse, he rode through the great forest to his next appointment, he espied three men standing in the road before him. When he rode up and saluted them politely they proceeded to take his horse by the bridle and tell him they are the men that he insulted in the meeting, and that they are going to whip him, and were not going to take the advantage of him. They had already cast lots and pointed out the man that was to give him the thrashing, and that the other two would see it well done, and that he should have fair play, ordering him to dismount and take his coat off and get ready.

He turned his eye on the one which was to give him the whipping, and still sitting on his horse, said to them all, "I want to thank you for the whipping before you give it, for they gave it to my Savior, Paul, Peter, and others, and I am delighted with the thought of walking in their footprints. The Lord in that meeting flooded us with glory, and I have heaven in my soul, and never was in so good a shape to receive a threshing as now." The appointee looked him in the face a minute or two, and said to his comrades: "Fellows, there is too much God in this man for me to put my hands on him, and I'm not going to do it; therefore if he gets a threshing you will have to give it to him."

They strived in vain to bolster him up. Finally all three coming to the same conclusion that there was too much God in the man for them to lay a hand on him. Then he proceeded to preach to them, pray for them, claimed them for the kingdom of God, and for preachers, and bidding them a loving adieu went on his way shouting the victory.

CHAPTER IV

REGENERATION

Regeneration is the grand *sine qua non* without which there is not a solitary ray of heavenly hope. John 3:7, "Ye must be born from above," not as E. V., "again," which Jesus never said, because *palin* means again and does not stand in this passage, but another, which has no meaning, but from above, as it is from *ana*, above and *then*, the regular adverbial termination in the Greek language. It positively and exclusively means from above, thus beautifully revelatory of the blessed fact that it came down from God, out of heaven, as it is the direct work of the Holy Spirit, wrought in the heart, creating the divine life in the dead human spirit.

Satan in his Edenic assault on Adam achieved the greatest victory of the ages, because the whole human race with the innumerable unborn millions and billions were created in Adam, Eve being no exception to the unity of humanity in Adam (1 Cor. 15:22), as she was not a *d novo* creation, but a metamorphism of Adam's rib, which was created with him. Adam, like everything else God made, "whose seed was in itself, was the seed of humanity and no subsequent creation, as God made everything competent to repeat itself infinitesimally.

Adam was competent to repeat himself *ad infinitum*, but could not transmit what he did not possess, which was spiritual life, lost in the fall, as God said, "In the day thou eatest thereof, thou shalt surely die."

Man is a trinity like God, consisting of spirit, which is really the man proper, and consists of the conscience (God's telephone), the will and the affections; the soul, consisting of the intellect, memory, judgment, and sensibilities, and the body, simply the tenement in which the soul, the animal life, abides during mortality, and will be the habitation of the spirit after glorification. 1 Cor. 15:51-55.

When God created him, he was simply an animal, consisting of the *psychee* (soul), and *sooma* (body), like all other animals, till God "breathed into his nostrils the breath of life and he became a living soul." Thus as the Hebrew *ruach* (spirit), shows that he imparted to him His own divine life, which Satan knocked out of him when he sinned, thus leaving him a spiritual corpse. Every human being is generated in him spiritually dead and consisting of mind and body, both a wrecked, debilitated state, but not dead.

While total depravity is the great fundamental Bible truth, it only applies to the human spirit, which God pronounces dead. Eph. 1:2, "You hath He quickened who were dead in trespasses and in sins." Here the word quickened is a very strong Greek compound, *zooeepoieese*, from *zooee*, life, and creates the divine life in the dead soul in regeneration, without which there can be no sanctification and no heaven. Heb. 12:14.

The only reason why so many nominal Christians oppose sanctification is because they have never been "born from above," and are deluded by the devil, blindfolded and led down to hell through the churches, as he ingeniously manipulates their good standing in the church to consummate their delusion and damnation. It is impossible for anyone to

be regenerated by the Holy Ghost and not long for
entire sanctification, which is the victory of the soul
in Jesus, giving us a sweet prelibation of heaven,
for which every true Christian sighs and cries.   I
sought it nineteen years, preaching fifteen of those
years, till the Lord gave it to me forty-nine years
ago, fiftten years antecedently of the ingress of the
Holiness Movement into Dixie Land, giving me the
shine, shout, and leaps which has been getting better ever since, even now, at the age of eighty-four,
making me young while I am old.   From the fact
that Satan knows that if he can defeat regeneration, he gets the soul, without defalcation.   Oh, how
he marshalled earth and hell and filled the world
with Catholic priests, Campbellite preachers, Mormon prophets, and other counterfeits, to delude the
people with their churchisms, eloquence, flatteries,
and priestcraft.   Thus they sidetrack, ditch, and
strand until they can dump them into hell.

You see in the above Scriptures how Nicodemus,
though a great doctor of divinity, was utterly ignorant of the supernatural birth, thinking that it was
something to be done to his body, responding to
Jesus, "How can a man be born when he is old?"
"Can he enter the second time into his mother's
womb and be born?"   Jesus responded, v. 6, "That
which is generated of depravity, and that which is
generated of spirit is spirit."   Thus showing clearly
that he had no allusion whatever to the human body,
but a pure spirituality, the body having nothing to
do with it, following with v. 7, "Marvel not that I
said unto you, ye must be born from above," and
not the E. V., "again," which would send to hell
every child that ever died before the physical birth.

Again means a repetition and would put the spiritual birth after the physical, and render it impossible for those dying before the physical birth ever to get it. Thus it will populate hell with more infants than all the seventeen hundred million people now on the globe.

But all this is relieved if you will just look at the beautiful Greek, which Jesus and His apostles preached. But *anthoothen* has no meaning but from above; thus knocking out the paganistic and Campbellite humbuggery of taking the people down to the river and putting their bodies in it, instead of climbing a sacred mountain with which the Bible abounds, Sinai, Calvary, Zion, Tabor, Carmel, Olivet, Pisgah, etc., on which God came down and revealed Himself to the patriarchs and prophets, thus showing the pertinency of climbing a mountain to find God instead of going down to the river.

I was preaching out in my old district, in Kentucky, where I was presiding elder forty years ago, when they came for me about forty miles and constrained me to let them carry me to their campmeeting, arriving after the preacher had begun his sermon. He said to his audience, "Brother Godbey has come, and as he will leave us so quickly I give way and let him now proceed to preaching." Ever since He gave me that wonderful baptism forty-nine years ago I have always been ready to preach and to die. So I proceeded and preached, announcing to them that I would have to leave on the one o'clock train the ensuing afternoon. Consequently they had me preach four solid hours the next morning, when I bade them a loving adieu. It so happened that I lodged with the evangelist conducting the meeting, who told me that he was born, reared and educated in a hotbed of Campbellism. He had gone to preaching without a knowledge of the Lord, who in His providence permitted him to hear some Holiness people preach on the streets, in His signal mercy using them to give him the light. He saw to his surprise that he had never been "born from above."

As he was a preacher he felt ashamed to become a public seeker. So he climbed a mountain, fell on his knees, lifted up his voice, "Oh, God! I have come hither to get you to come down and save my soul and shall never leave till you do—will stay here praying and starve to death, and somebody will come along and find a pile of bones." If you think you can get ahead of God you are awfully mistaken, or get Him into a corner, He will always run on you a glorious surprise. So he said, before he was aware, he found himself jumping as high as he could and making the mountain roar and reverberate with shouts of victory, waking up to the ecstatic realization that God had actually answered his prayer, saved his soul, and he enjoyed the ineffable felicity of the supernatural birth.

He then pretty soon in His good providence went to a meeting and heard Andrew Johnson, our brilliant Holiness evangelist, preach on sanctification, rushed to the altar, received it gloriously and arose shouting like an angel. He went to his church shouting and thinking surely they would be delighted with the good news. He went away to a two weeks' meeting, and returning, was informed that in his absence they had held a church meeting, pronounced him crazy, turned him out of the ministry and out of the membership. He said to me, "Brother God-bey, I am no 'come-outer,' I believe in the church, but have no membership anywhere on the face of the earth." So I accommodated him by receiving him into the Nazarene Church, as I am the oldest preacher in the Holiness Movement on the earth and represent it in all of its organizations.

Jesus goes on with Nicodemus, v. 8, "The Spirit breathes on whom He will; thou hearest His voice, but cans't not tell whence He cometh nor whither He goeth, even so is everyone who is born of the Spirit;" thus showing up the pure spirituality of this birth, having nothing to do with the human body and not a drop of material water in a million miles of it. The Bible was never divided into chapters and verses by the inspired writers. This was done by the London printers, in 1551, as a matter of their own convenience in handling it, just as you see my books are all chaptered and paragraphed as a matter of necessity for the printers. Therefore wink at the fourth chapter division of John's Gospel, and you run at once into our Savior's next sermon. In this He had a lonely auditor; at the opposite pole of the social battery, as Nicodemus was at the front and the Samaritan down at the bottom of slumdom.

Jesus mentioned water only once to Nicodemus, but seven times to the poor fallen woman at Jacob's well, who naturally concluded that He meant the water in the well for which she had walked a mile. This well, ninety feet deep, has the finest of pure limpid water which I have often drunk. He told her twice over emphatically that she was mistaken, at the same time certifying positively that He meant "living water," i. e., the water of life, Himself.

Your see clearly and indubitably the mistake of the woman which Jesus so emphatically corrected twice, saying, "The well is deep and you have no windlass and cannot draw it." Thus He positively certified repeatedly that He is not talking about the water in the well, but the water of life, which, those who drink will never thirst again. As he proceeds preaching to her the blessed Gospel, she is reminded of what she had heard, "That a Messiah cometh who will teach us all things." He responds at once, "I am He. Go call your husband." She said she had none. Oh, how beautiful and simple the Messianic and apostolic preaching! He knew all about her and that she was a poor prostitute, down at the bottom. We should remember in all our preaching to emulate the example of Jesus and the apostles, who always shot to kill, i. e., aiming at the heart.

So the ammunition had the desired effect, so to convict her that she confessed outright, "I have no husband," when He proceeded to tell her that the one she had was her fifth, yet not her husband. We only have a few words of this wonderful sermon which Jesus preached to the lonely prostitute, so low down that the cultured clergy would not look at her. God help us all to follow His own example and neglect nobody. The normal conclusion deduced from the context, as you see, when you read this Scripture, is that she got just what Jesus was talking about, i. e., the water of life, which is Himself, and Himself alone. Every soul failing to get it is forever lost. "In Christ shall all be made alive;" not the devil's false doctrine of Universalism, Russellism, or any other phase of nohellism, because the glorious vicarious atonement does reach every human being.

This poor heathen woman had heard the thrilling message that God was going to send the Messiah into the world, to teach us the Great truth of salvation and deliver us from all the horrific evils incident to this life, and restore us back to the beauty and purity we lost in the fall. When He notified her that she has actively met and is now conversing with that long-expected Messiah the Holy Spirit prevails, and unhesitatingly she says yes to the Holy Ghost, believes His precious word and enters into the kingdom of God. She is born from above, powerfully converted, to her infinite delight finding herself a joyful partaker of the water of life which Jesus alone can give.

Then forgetting the water in Jacob's well, for which she had walked a mile, and the vessel she had brought, she dashed off at race horse speed. She runs, shouting jubilantly, and telling everybody that she had found the Christ whom the world had wanted four thousand years, and He had gloriously saved her soul, filling her with heavenly bliss. The people crowded around her, astounded and spellbound, to see and hear the worst woman in the city preaching the Gospel. They clamor on all sides. "O, do show us that wonderful Christ, for whom the world has waited so long." Now she says, "Follow me." They delightedly crowd after her in thronging multitudes, everyone that hears the shout dropping his work, running away and joining the procession. They march away to Jacob's well to see that wonderful prophet who had told the woman all her life, and demonstrated His messiahship by gloriously saving her soul, and changing her into a flaming preacher of the Gospel.

The multitude hangs on His eloquent lips spellbound, the two days of His abiding, many believing on Him and heroically corroborating the thrilling testimony of the unutterable sweetness of the living water which Jesus gave them. Truly He is the water of life, the Bible old and new confirms. Isaiah 55th ch., "So everyone that thirsteth come ye to the waters, flowing freely, without money, and without price." That chapter is all about Christ (as Isaiah was the great Messianic prophet, incessantly preaching the coming Christ, seven hundred years prior to the Bethlehem birth), that Himself is the water of life, freely flowing for all to drink and live is inevitable and no allusion whatever to material water.

The woman thought that He meant the water in the well, and reminding Him He had no way of drawing it up those ninety feet, He proceeded so lucidly to correct her mistake, telling her twice that He did not mean the water in the well, but living water, which she actually received in her poor dead soul, when she believed the beautiful truth which He enunciated. He so gloriously converted her soul, and despite her awfully wicked life, armed her with the commission to preach the Gospel.

These discourses of our Savior to Nicodemus and the Samaritan woman clearly show up and warrant the conclusion that there is not a drop of water in the regeneration which the Holy Ghost administers to the human heart when He creates the divine life in the dead human spirit.

When a little boy I heard my sainted mother sing so much a song I never can forget:

"The richest man I ever saw,
    Was the one that begged the most,
    For he was always full of Jesus,
    And the Holy Ghost."

Followed by the chorus—

"And to begging I will go."

Begging means praying, as this was always praying to Jesus and the Holy Ghost. Rest assured, in
these Scriptures, "born of water and Spirit," simply
means born of Jesus and the Holy Ghost. We all
know that Jesus alone is the water of life and the
Holy Ghost, the only Spirit in the plan of salvation,
therefore when He regenerates He simply creates
the life of Jesus in you, so you are actually that
very moment born of water and spirit, John 3:5.
God is omnipotent, He needs no help to do His work,
therefore when you run off after preachers and mill-
ponds to save your soul, you go headlong into idolatry, which is so abominable in the sight of God.
In the Bible it is currently cognomened "abomination."

Many unconverted and backslidden preachers in
the great orthodox churches so lamentably deceive
multiplied millions, preaching to them water baptism essential to regeneration, instead of Jesus only,
who is the water of life, created in the heart by the
Holy Ghost. He superinduces the supernatural
birth, which all must receive or lose their souls.
Hence, you perceive, the fond advice of Satan, flooding the world with his false prophets, constituting
the vast majority of popular preachers. They lull
to sleep the guilty consciences of the poor deluded
people, who blindly follow them. They comfort them

in life, and preach eloquent funeral sermons over them when they die, assuring their bereaved friends that they are then in heaven, when in hell, like Dives (Luke 16:23), "who lifted up his eyes in hell, being in torment."

As the Protestant churches were organized in the dawn of our civlization, on the retreat of the Dark Ages, a thousand years, during which not one man in a thousand, nor one woman in twenty thousand, could read, idolatry and priestcraft filled the inhabited earth; ignorance, superstition and crime superabounded, and the church actually retrogressed, except a persecuted martyr here and there. The beautiful spiritual truth of the Bible was totally eclipsed by the dense clouds of ignorance, and superstition, idolatry, heresy, everywhere. These so dominated the popular mind, till Christianity shone as a dim taper, which needed snuffing.

The creeds of the popular churches were formulated during the foggy ingress of the brilliant civilization, which in the providence of God we are permitted to enjoy. It is high time we should be coming back to the blessed Bible which shouts the victory. Especially is it important that we reach solid Bible truths, on the grand fundamentals of the redemptive scheme, regeneration and sanctification. We should never say "born again," as Jesus never said it; but "born from above," and eliminate forever the old dark age dogma "that born of water" has any allusion whatever to water baptism; Jesus is the water of life, mentioned in these Scriptures. Therefore, it means to be born of Jesus and the Holy Ghost.

6

CHAPTER V

SANCTIFICATION

When Lucifer, the great archangel, fell from heaven long ago (Isa. 14:12. "How thou art fallen, O Lucifer, the sun of the morning"), he lost his hold on God and was separated from Him. Thus carnality entered heaven. When fallen Lucifer, *i. e.*, the devil, was cast out of heaven (Rev., 12th ch.). "The dragon's tail drew after him one-third of the stars and hurled them down from heaven, *i. e.*, Satan's influence drew one-third of the angels which were cast out of heaven and became demons, which now fill hell and throng the atmosphere of this world. God lost one-third of His angels when Lucifer fell, and no wonder He has decreed, Heb. 12:14, "Without sanctification no one shall see the Lord."

The meaning of sanctification is to take out of the heart the depravity which we all inherited from Adam through the fall. 1 Cor. 15:22, "In Adam all die." Psa. 51:5, "Lord, I am vile, conceived in sin, born unholy and unclean; sprung from the man whose guilty fall corrupts his race and ruins all." Hence, we see there is no possibility of any human soul ever getting into heaven without entire sanctification. *Hagiasmos*, from *gee*, "the world," and *alpha*, "not," and consequently it means to take the world out of you, 1 John 3:16. All this is the world, "the lust of flesh, the lust of the eye and the pride of life," which constitutes the unholy trinity, antithetical to God's trinity, Father, Son, and Holy Ghost. Satan's trinity must be eliminated from the heart, for it is certain we will never enter heaven. This is the reason the devil hates sanctification worse than anything else, and fights it under all circumstances, resorting to all sorts of devices and stratagems to keep people from ever seeking it, and when they get it, it turns all hell loose against them to cheat them out of it.

Satan is awfully upset and disappointed when a sinner is converted, because he then loses his crop, which is swept away by the swelling river of the supernatural birth, inundating the soul, and utterly bankrupting him. Yet his indefatigable perseverance rallies his myrmidons, to concentrate all their forces and get him to backslide, plunge headlong into sin, till he is worse than he ever was before. The deadly upas tree having been cut down by the Gospel axe, sprouts out from the roots, one hundred instead of one, which will soon grow into trees, prolific of damnatory fruit, for the enrichment of hell. But when the man instead of backsliding pushes forward heroically into sanctification, he is utterly impoverished because he loses his form, which is the inbred sin hereditary in every heart, without which no one can commit actual transgression, fall under condemnation and lose his soul.

Satan hates sanctification worse than anything; and lies under contribution all the chicanery of the pandemonium, to keep people from seeking it and defeat all their efforts to get it. When they will, despite his devices, seek importunately, sighing and crying night and day, as I did nineteen years, he will if possible discourage them, so they give it up. Yet when they persevere and get it despite all his efforts to head them off, then he resorts to all sorts of strate-

gems to derail, sidetrack, ditch, strand, and get them
into his counterfeit, and thus utterly cheat them out
of their sweet and rich experience of perfect love
and a clean heart, utterly grieving away the Holy
Spirit and ripening them for the bottomless pit.

His most plausible device is to run them after
a third blessing, as in the present Holiness Movement he had them go off after power, using Acts
1:8, "You shall receive power after the Holy Ghost
has come upon you," a wrong translation, as the true
reading gives, "you shall receive the power of the
Holy Ghost having come on you." The Holy Ghost
Himself the only power.

Hence, if you go off after some other power, Satan will give it to you and win you forever. The
second great movement which Satan used was a
third blessing of fire, after Jesus has baptized you
with the Holy Ghost and fire. This opens wide the
door for the devil to give you hell fire, and his false
prophets to give you wildfire and foxfire; the *ignis
fatems*, whose delusive rays light up unreal worlds
and glows but to betray. The last and most calami-
tous assault hell has made against the Holiness
Movement, is the departure after the gift of tongues.
Its votaries have no tongue, but simply noises, like
frogs and birds, imparted by evil spirits, which cannot give you a language, but gibberish, characteristic of the false prophets of all ages. Isa. 8:19,
"The wizards who peep and mutter."

This "tongue movement" has proved horrifically
detrimental to the dear Holiness people, lassoing so
many of them, leading them away into wild fanati-
cisms so they have lost their experiences, grieved
away the Holy Spirit. Many of them even plunged

headlong deep into sin, even committing crimes
against the civil law and going into the penitentiary
to exploit their follies and gross iniquities, like the
dog in Æsops Fables, walking through the river
with a piece of meat in his mouth, and seeing his
own shadow in the water, he thought it was another
dog, with a piece of meat in his mouth. He jumped
at him to take it from him, and opening his mouth
to get it, let go his own piece, which the swift river
carries away. As there was no dog nor meat, but
he had seen his own shadow, he was left without
any meat, having lost what he had.

That is precisely what the devil does with all the
Holiness people who go off after a third blessing.
They grieve the Holy Spirit away and lose their san-
tification. There is no third blessing for them to
get, because the Holy Ghost has only three great
works of grace, in the salvation of the soul, regeneration for the sinner, giving him a new heart, and
sanctification for the Christian, giving him a clean
heart, and glorification for the dying saints, sweeping away all infirmities in the article of death, simultaneously with the evacuation of the body by the immortal soul.

All efforts to get another work of grace after
sanctification are superinduced by Satan and his
myrmidons, in their diversified caprices to cheat
people of their sanctification, as they know that it
is their only possible hope of securing their damnation.

"Is it possible Brother Godbey, that we can get
no blessing after we are sanctified till we die?" San-
tification is full salvation, crucifying the old man of
sin, taking him out of the heart, and filling you with

the Holy Ghost; actually giving you Christian perfection, which is really entire sanctification. It is from *facio*, to make, and *per*, complete, and consequently means to give you a complete work of grace, while sanctification is from that same word *facio*, to make, and *sanctus*, holy, and thus you see they mean one and the same work of grace, and the last one we can get in this life. Yet you must remember the Bible describes the land of Canaan, peculiarized by frequent showers falling, irrigating fields and gardens, making it flow with milk and honey, abound in corn and wine, and all the delicious fruits and superabounding in luxuries, giving us a copious living of royal bounty.

Sanctification is in its very nature paradoxically growthy. We see the lovely innocent lamb and it grows to be an elephant, as I have seen them in India, weighing 10,000 pounds. It begins a bright, limpid inexhaustible flowing fountain, swells into a majestic river, broadens into a beautiful crystal sea and magnifies into an ocean without bank or bottom; even the grim monster having no power to mar the glorious heavenly prelibation, thus flowing in the enraptured soul.

> "Why should we start and fear to die.
>   What timorous worms we mortals are!
> Death is the gate of endless joy,
>   And yet we dread to enter there!
>
> "Oh, that my Lord would come and meet,
>   My soul would stretch her wings in haste,
> Fly fearless through death's iron gate,
>   Nor feel the terrors as she past."

While the sanctified experience is the felicitous Canaan life, wonderful for all conceivable spiritual growth and development out of pigmyhood into gianthood, replete with glorious victories over the world, the flesh, and Satan. We flourish like trees planted by the river side, spreading out their branches like the green bay trees. When we evacuate these mortal tenements and pass the pearly portals into the new Jerusalem, thus exchanging labor for rest, the cross for the crown, earth for heaven, we will actually get religion faster than ever before. Everything there will be in our favor, to help us on our grand march to loftier altitudes, broader and deeper experiences than ever before. "This world is no friend to grace, to help us on to God." And here we sing:

"How tedious and tasteless the hours,
    When Jesus no longer I see,
Sweet prospects, sweet birds, and sweet flowers,
    Have all lost their sweetness to me.

The midsummer sun shines but dim,
    The fields strive in vain to look gay,
But when I am happy in Him,
    December's as pleasant as May.

I would, were He always thus nigh,
    Have nothing to wish or to fear;
No mortal so happy as I.
    My summer would last all the year.

Oh, drive these dark clouds from my sky,
    Thy soul-cheering presence rest o'er,
Or take me up to Thee on high,
    Where winter and clouds are no more."

In heaven all move in the same direction, God-ward and Holinessward, unutterably delighted to do God's will. Thus eternally progressive in the divine similitude, swimming in a boundless ocean of perfect love, amid the transcendent felicities of the heavenly universities, taught by angels, archangels, cherubims, seraphims, heavenly hierarchies, environed by the patriots and prophets, saints and martyrs, whose teaching we deliciously enjoyed in the blessed Bible. They preceded us thousands of years and enjoyed all the wonderful heavenly society, and will far eclipse themselves in Biblical lore. Oh, what wonderful progress we will make.

I once in my travels picked up a book in a Christian home, "Scenes Beyond the Grave," by Mayetta Davis, Elmy, N. Y. On the title page were the affidavits of her pastor of the Baptist Church, and her physician, certifying to the truth of the book, stating that she had died and been put in a vault, and had revived the ninth day, having been to heaven. She then wrote the contents of the book, stating what she saw, giving an account of the nursery in which all infants were taught by the angels. They made such wonderful progress as to become the teachers of their own parents when they arrived in heaven. She certified that all heaven is a wonderful school, in which all are deeply interested as teachers and students.

While Satan makes an awful fight against regeneration, yet when it comes to sanctification he actually must call his hosts on earth and in hell against the people to keep them from seeking sanctification. In the case of Pharaoh, who symbolizes the devil, he did his best to hold Israel in bondage at every cost, and when he could not keep them from leaving his country, begged them not to go very far, so he could fetch them back again. The reason why the popular churches are so opposed to sanctification is simply the Satanic influence among them. The very powers of hell are combined to hold them back, as they know in that case they have succeeded in dragging them into hell.

You can see in the E. V. the translators were not sanctified and looked upon it as a blessing only for a saint in an age, and which they could only get by seeking it a long time. Hebrews, 6th ch., leaving the beginning of the Gospel of Christ. Let us go on to perfection, should read, let us be carried to perfection, as the Greek is *pheroometha,* from *phreoo,* to carry, and does not mean go at all. They had no right to so translate it, but took the liberty to put it down, because they thought in order to be a perfect Christian we had to live a long time, work hard, and suffer much, whereas the verb is in the present tense, imperative mood, beautifully revealing the consolatory fact that Jesus our Sanctifier is standing by us, just ready to take us in His arms and carry us into the experience, leaving us nothing to do but bid Satan an eternal adieu, giving back to him everything we ever got from him, making the complete consecration.

A squatter in the swamps in Arkansas shaking with the ague, sees a traveler walking by. Looking out of his window he shouts to him, "Whither goest thou?" It so happened he was a Christian man and responded, "I am going to heaven." When he asked, "How long have you been on the road?" he said, "Forty years." Then he responded, "If you have traveled forty years and only got as far as Arkansas, I think you had better give it up, as you will never get there."

The churches abound in weary pilgrims who have traveled forty years and have only gotten as far as the aguey swamps of Arkansas. Their testimonies are so discouraging that only one now and then reaches Beulahland, despite the Lord's appeal constantly ringing in their ears. (1 Thes. 4:3. This is His will, your sanctification.)   E. V., there has "even," which the translators put in.   An adverb of surprise, because they thought it was such a wonder and only one here and there could get it; whereas the Lord positively said that He has willed it to every Christian.   We have nothing to do but take it and thank the Giver, shout the victory over the flesh, the world and the devil, go on our way rejoicing, singing jubilantly:

"I have found a friend in Jesus,
    He is everything to me,
The fairest of ten thousand to my soul,
    The lily of the valley,

The bright and morning star,
    The fairest of ten thousand to my soul.
He all my griefs has taken,
    And all my sorrow borne,

He tells me every care on Him to roll.
    I have all for him forsaken,
And all the idols from my heart have torn,
    And now He keeps me by His power,

Though all the world forsake me,
  And Satan tempt me sore.
Through Jesus I shall safely reach the goal,
  He will never, never leave me,

Nor yet forsake me here,
  While I live by faith and do his blessed will;
A wall of fire around me,
  I have nothing now to fear.

With His manna
  He my hungry soul shall fill!
Then sweeping up to glory,
  We shall see His blessed face.

When rivers of delight shall ever roll.
  He is the lily of the valley,
The bright and morning star,
  The fairest of ten thousand to my soul!"

The reason why I sought it nineteen years, and many others seek it so long, is because there are three "F"s" in every experience we receive from God, whether the justification, the sanctification of a Christian or the healing of the body; the first "F" is faith; the second, fact, and the third, feeling. Satan adroitly turns them around, putting feeling first, then the fact, and last of all he will let you believe it, thus utterly upsetting the whole enterprise, as you cannot feel it tlll you get it. Thus the devil stirs up every seeker to look for feeling, when he has nothing to feel, and consequently floods him with discouragement, oblivious of God's loving call:

"Come humble sinner, in whose breast
　　A thousand thoughts revolve,
Come with your guilt and fears oppressed,
　　And make this last resolve.

I go to Jesus though my sins,
　　Have like a mountain rose,
I know His courts, I'll enter in,
　　Whatever may oppose."

Prostrate I lie before His throne,
　　And there my guilt confess.
I'll tell Him I'm a wretch undone,
　　Without His sovereign grace.

I can but perish if I go,
　　I am resolved to try,
But if I stay away I know
　　I must forever die."

Oh, now Jesus pleads with you now. "All the fitness He requireth is to feel your need of Him." This He gives you, now is the accepted time, now is the day of salvation, while you hear His voice harden not you heart.

All we have to do is to leave the devil forever, fully give up to God, for this world and all others, and in case of the sinner radically repent of all his sins so he will not commit them again, but die in his tracks rather than commit another sin. Then and there believe that God for Jesus' sake forgives the past and He always does it responsively to your faith, as He cannot fail because His word is as solid as His throne.

The sinner gives up all his bad things to the devil in order to leave him forever, at once going for a radical repentance accompanied by profound contrition, confession and restitution. The Christian in his consecration for sanctification gives up to God all his good things, with the distinct understanding that He abides with Him forever.

1 Pet. 2:1-4, "Having laid aside all malice, all guile, hypocrisies, caluminations, as newly born babes, long after sincere milk of the word, that you may grow thereby unto salvation if you have tasted that the Lord is good, to whom going forth as to a living stone, rejected by men, but with God's elect and precious, you yourselves are built up a spiritual family, a royal priesthood, offering up spiritual sacrifice unto God, acceptable through Jesus Christ." In this beautiful and comprehensive passage by the senior apostle we have lucidly set forth the full consecration of the Christian, in the utter abandonment of all phases of inbred sin, thus putting him on believing ground to receive the experience by simple appropriative faith. Here we see we are to utterly abandon all Satanic guile and hypocrisies whereas Paul recognizes Holy guile, "Being crafty I caught you with guile." Hence, we see that we are to be "as wise as serpents and as harmless as doves," faithfully and heroically bring into availability all our gifts and graces, so freely and richly conferred by the Holy Ghost; saved by the latter, "Love, joy, peace, long-suffering, gentleness, goodness, faith, meekness, holiness" (Gal. 5:22), and save others by the former, wisdom, knowledge, faith, bodily-healing, the working of gospel miracles, prophecy, dis-

cernment of spirit, tongues, and the interpretation
of tongues, 1 Cor. 12:8-11.

Forty-eight years ago while chopping wood for
my dear wife a man rode up on a horse, leading another and said, "Brother Godbey, Brother Bruner
(a Baptist pastor with 400 members) has sent
me to bring you to Deep Creek to help him in a revival meeting." I responded, "I am sorry, I cannot
go, I am so crowded with work." He said, "Antici-
pating something of that kind, he ordered me never
to come back without you." I knew then God was
in it and said, "Dismount, go in the house and take
a chair, and as soon as I can change my apparel I
will be off with you." We darted away twelve miles
on the fleet horses. It was an old style August meeting, beginning at 10 A.M., holding on all day, with
dinner on the ground, free for all; not a cent paid
for the good dinner and delicious fruits which
abounded. His 400 members, augmented by the multitude coming for the loaves and fishes, gave us a
great audience. He met me in the yard and with
flowing tears said, "Brother Godbey, I am so glad
you have come, Brother Sherley (a big Baptist
preacher) and myself have preached with all our
might ten days, and have not seen a tear, or heard
a groan; I have been pastor twenty years and my
church seems to have died on my hands; my heart is
broken, I have more than I can bear. I feel that I
will die unless I see a revival in my church. I never
heard you preach, but I know you have revivals
everywhere you go, and that is what I want and
must have. I turn over the meeting to you, and will
amen all your preaching, and will help you the best
I can in everything you do."

Thus feeling free as Gabriel, leaving him and his helper in the pulpit, I walked out in front, took my text from John the Baptist and preached to them with all my might, proving everything by that wonderful preacher, whom they claim as the founder of their church (though I knew he was not, but did not tell them so). I said not a word about John Wesley, but with my stentorian voice roared out the beautiful truths, preached so heroically by John the Baptist. Matt. 3:11, "I indeed baptize you with water unto repentance, but He that cometh after me will baptize you with Holy Ghost and fire." The Campbellites had overrun the country with their idolatrous water doctrine, giving those orthodox Baptists awful trouble. So I said, "I am glad you have been converted and baptized with water, but you see if you stop on the water line you are not Baptists but only Campbellites. Therefore, if you would be orthodox in the succession of your noble founder, you must get Jesus to baptize you with the Holy Ghost and fire." Thus pleading with all my might, I opened the altar both for Christians to seek the baptism which Jesus gives and sinners to seek salvation. Hitherto there had been no move in the congregation. They rushed from all directions into the altar, and piled up a pellmell mass, as there were so many anxious to seek the Lord. I exhorted them to go to praying with all their might, assuring them that God would verify His promises, save the sinners and sanctify the Christians. They heroically took me at my word, and soon some were on their feet shouting aloud, and a wonderful revival thus broke out and swept like a cyclone.

I could only stay five days. I opened the door of the Baptist Church and forty grown men and women who had been gloriously converted rushed forward and gave the pastor and myself their hands as candidates for membership. When I was about to leave some of them appealed to me in these words, "Brother Godbey, since you have been among us we have been much exercised in prayer in reference to the pastorate of our church, which Brother Bruner has occupied for twenty years. We all love him like a father, but praying over it we have reached the conclusion that a change will be for the glory of God, and all want you to become pastor of our church." I responded, "Brethren, do you not know that I am a Methodist preacher," when they responded, "We certainly do, but know another thing, and that is you have preached the Baptist doctrine better than we ever heard it before and we want you for our pastor." I said, "Brethren, they would excommunicate you from their association if you take me for your pastor." When they said, "We will take chances on that, as we propose, led by the Lord, to manage our own affairs."

Of course, I would not get them into trouble, consequently I blessed them all, and bade them adieu. Hence, you see, like Paul, I caught them all with guile, not deflecting an iota from the straight Bible truth, but simply rendering John the Baptist exceedingly prominent in my ministry. I did this in all good conscience, because he is the model for us all, as he ignored his own personality, only claiming to be a "voice" for God. Therefore, that wonderful baptism which Jesus gave me forty-nine years ago burned up the Free Mason, the Odd Fellow, college president, and Southern Methodist preacher, leaving me nothing but a radical Free Methodist, delighted to walk in the footprints of John the Baptist. All human creeds were burned up by the fire of the Holy Ghost and leaving me simply a voice for God, faithfully and fearlessly telling the people everywhere the beautiful truths by which we are saved, sanctified, fed and panoplied, and by which we will be judged in the great day.

About a dozen years ago, while the yellow fever was raging on the Gulf Coast, having broken out terrifically in New Orleans, in the midst of the grand Alma Mater camp-meeting at Scottsville, Texas, a group of well dressed men suddenly appeared walking down the central aisle of the great tabernacle with the tread of authority, magnetizing the multitude. They deliberately mounted the rostum with the preachers and choir, and taking possession of the situation, in the name of the city board of health, pronounced the encampment adjourned *sine die,* asking the pastor to pronounce the benediction. They explained their autocratic procedure was in order to prevent the spread of the awful contagion, which had broken out in New Orleans.

Evangelist Ruth and your humble servant, the preachers called to run the camp with many others, at once fled to the depot to make our escape out of the country into the disinfected North, where the panic would not break up our meetings. Soon we were aboard the train, northern bound. The conductor came along and took our tickets, soon followed by another man in uniform, demanding our health certificates, which Ruth and myself had for-

7

tunately procured from the board,. and consequently moved on all right; meanwhile many on that
crowded train were without health certificates. The
man demanding the certificates represented Mississippi, into which we would soon run, and as it was
quarantined against Texas, and all the Gulf Coast,
he ordered them all to get off the train. They positively refused, observing that they had paid for their
run. Consequently we ran along an hour, when we
found ourselves halted amid a great forest, afar
from a depot. Looking around we see armed men
on horses, who at once dismounted, entered the train
and disembarked everyone who could not show a
health certificate.

In a similar manner when I was preaching in
India, running from Bombay, the million metropolis
of central India, to Madras, the largest city in the
great South, we found the long train (as in that
country thousand travel as the hundreds do in this),
halted and everybody ordered to disembark, and
stand while physicians came along and diagnosed us
all in reference to plague symptoms, as the whole
province of Madras was quarantined against that
of Bombay, because the plague there killed the people all the time, suddenly falling and dying in one
to five minutes, the medical world having searched
in vain for a remedy. While preaching in that city
every day showed up in the city papers the fright-
ful death roll. While they passed me, they halted not
a few, permitting none to run into the province of
Madras without a health certificate.

Justification is really a through ticket to heaven,
as God has decreed, "Without the sanctification no
one shall see the Lord." Therefore we will all find

the gates of heaven fortified by guardian angels, with swords crossed, above the pearly portals, because heaven is quarantined against all this world, every atom of which is contaminated by Satan's pestiferous tread. Therefore, rest assured that no soul will ever enter without the health certificate, which is none other than a clean heart, entire sanctification, which Jesus alone can give. He is always ready and delighted to baptize all the Father's children with the Holy Ghost and fire, giving a clean heart, the shine, the shout and the leap, the victory forever.

CHAPTER VI.

DEEPER THINGS

1 Peter 4:10, "The God of all grace having called you to His eternal glory, will make you perfect, having suffered a little while will establish you, strengthen and settle you." King James' translation thought it meant physical suffering; whereas the whole sentence is pre-eminently spiritual and signifies the crucifixion of the old man. Romans 6:6, and Colossians 2:11.

It simply means that we are to suffer long enough for old Adam to die, which is really but a moment, as Wesley says, "Though the man on the cross may long suffer and bleed, hours and even days, yet he dies in a moment,," just as I am traveling through Ohio toward Indiana, approaching it every step, yet I cross the line in a moment, perhaps incognito, and find myself in Hoosierdom.

Now you see this wondreful experience of Christian perfection, which is entire sanctification, is received in a moment when the impersonality dies. We see it lucidly illustrated in the death of Agog, king of the Amaleckites, whom Samuel, the brilliant type of Christ, cut to pieces with his sword. He symbolized the old man of sin in every human heart, whom we cannot take to heaven with us, and unless destroyed will prove Satan's millstone dragging us down to hell and sinking us eternally into a deeper damnation, as hell has no bottom. We may seek sanctification ever so long, and still when it comes we receive it in a moment.

"In a twinkling of an eye,
Jesus' blood can sanctify;
The cleansing stream I see,
I plunge and, lo, it cleanseth me;
I rise to walk in heaven's own light,
Above the world of sin,
With heart made pure and garments white,
And Christ enthroned within."

The reason it took me so long to get sanctified was because there were no Holiness people to tell me how to consecrate fully, which we can do in a moment, when we forever turn over to God all we know and all we do not know and believe His word. Matt. 23:19, "The altar sanctifies the gift." You are the gift, and Christ the altar, Hebrew 13:10. When you have nothing to do but shout the victory and be true, as God's word is as solid as His throne. "This is the victory that overcometh the world, even our faith."

The reason why people find it so hard to get the experience of entire sanctification is because Satan knows that if they get it he is eternally defeated. Consequently he adroitly reverses the three "F's" in sanctification; first, faith; then, fact, and last of all, feelings, which never can come till we get it. Therefore Satan turns the problem round, putting the feeling first and then the fact, and last of all he lets you believe it. In this way he kept me in the howling wilderness nineteen years, trying to feel it when I had nothing to feel. Finally I ventured to take it by faith, without any feeling, when He soon turned a Niagara down on me, giving me more feeling than I knew what to do with, rolling like a heavenly river, flooding my soul, spreading into a beautiful crystal sea, broadening out into a majestic ocean without bank or bottom, in which I have been floating and diving these forty-nine years, getting richer and sweeter as the fugitive years speed their flight.

Here you see four great and important works of grace, perfection, establishment, invigoration and settlement; the latter three, the normal successors of the great second work, constituting the glorious positive hemisphere of the sanctified experience; the cleansing of the heart from inbred sin by the Holy Ghost. He is the Custodian and Administrator of the cleansing blood, which He always applies to the expurgation of all inbred sin out of the heart, making it pure, clean and holy. That He is willing to enter in the blessed and glorious paraclyte, giving us constant victory over the world, the flesh and the devil, a sweet prelibation of heaven, thus making life a glorious sunshine and perfectly harmonical with God, singing out one eternal yes to His sweet will, actually bringing down

> Heaven our souls to greet,
> While glory crowns the mercy seat.

The Bible, old and new, illustrates our wonderful Christanity by trees and houses. We see it in its beauty and glory (Psa., 1st ch.). God blessed man, "a tree planted by the river of water, bringing forth his fruit in his season," his leaf is always green, and his life a glorious victory, in contradistinction to the ungodly, who are like the chaff which the winds carry away.

The redwood tree (*taxodium genus*) in California (which I have often seen not only in its native land, but in the British Museum in London), certified by counting his growth, to be six thousand years old was actually on the earth in the days of Adam, and has lived ever since. While its gigantic trunk towers above the clouds, its tenacious roots interpenetrate the soil, clay, soapstone, slate, and coil around the great strata, over which the subterranean rivers eternally flow; a triumphant fortification against the long summer drouth, amid which its neighbors perish for the needed irrigation and fall to the earth.

In the Bible "deep" and "high" are synonymous; these wonderful experiences of full salvation are beautifully illustrated by these magnitudinous roots, interpenetrating far down, and winding round the very foundation of the earth, drinking from the rivers that never run dry. The imperial eagle soars far above all the storms and basks in the golden beams of an unsetting sun, as he wings his flight around the world, eating his breakfast in America and his dinner in Africa (Psa., 40th ch.). Those who rest in the Lord shall swap off their strength, *i. e.*, as our strength is nothing but weakness we swap it off for His almighty strength, which enables us to soar like eagles, run and not get weary, walk and not faint.

My father was a successful fruit culturist. He always, when he planted out a tree, put down a stake and tied it to it, so when its thick foliage gathered the winds, they would not be able to eradicate it. Thus we should always give especial attention to young Christians, keeping them into close identity with the old and strong. When our Savior (John,

21st ch.), after His resurrection, met His apostles
on the sea of Galilee, personating Peter, the senior
and representative of his comrades, He charged him
especially to shepherdize, *i. e.*, feed and protect the
lambs and sheeplings. *Probatia,* which means the
young sheep; the E. V. does not bring it out, but
mentions sheep twice; whereas the original specifies
lambs and sheeplings, as well as the grown sheep.

Railroad men in Boston united and built a depot
at the cost of a million dollars and proceeded at once
to occupy it, when to their surprise and mortifica-
tion they found the walls cracking and saw that it
was about to fall down. Consequently they had to
right about face, take it all down, lift out the foundation and go down deeper and rebuild it all.
Our Lord was the most simple, lucid and efficient
preacher on the earth, the model for us all, He used
the most common things we meet in domestic, social
and public life to illustrate the beautiful truths by
which all the people in the world are to be saved
and made sure of heaven, world without end, after
we die, from the simple fact that we have heaven
in the heart when we leave the world, and the blessed
Book assures us that there is no change, after we
wind up our probation, "As the tree falleth so shall
it be, whether it fall toward the north or the south."
This illustrates the absolute necessity of a solid
foundation. When they built the great suspension
bridge across the Mississippi at St. Louis they obli-
gated the company to sink all the pillars till the
steel tools struck fire, which meant to go down be-
low all the soapstone and slate and reach the grand
stratum on which God built the continents and
poured out the great oceans and spread the thun-

dering seas over the earth. They got down so deep that they could not reach them with vitalizing air, and men were lifted up dead, sending panic to all the laborers, so they had to pay a dollar an hour for work. They soon looked in the face of bankruptcy, and plead with their employers to rescind the contract and let them proceed building the pillars, but found them absolutely inflexible, consequently the company had to go into bankruptcy and receive a successor, which pushed the work vigorously till they reached the solid flint indubitably revealed by the flashing scintillations.

Jesus says, "The children of this world are wiser in their generation than the children of light." It should not be so. In many respects we can learn wisdom from the children of this world, who are so aggressive, redoubtable and indefatigable in their enterprises. As they persevered despite the terror of the grim monster, till they saw the material fire flash, we should always press on fearlessly of howling demons and the frowning world, till Jesus baptizes with the Holy Ghost and fire, and sends us out singing the shout. "Oh, the blessing and the power that the Lord gave me then, for I never can forget how the fire fell when He sanctified me."

Each work of grace is a beautiful spiritual globe, in the supernatural birth justification constituting the negative hemisphere, giving you a clear record in heaven, while regeneration, the positive hemisphere, gives you a new heart; yet only a newly born babe, with the grand problem of spiritual manhood, reaching till vision is eclipsed by the blue ether, revealing infinitesimal possibilities of development and achievement sweeping on through the lapse of endless ages. It not only culminates in sanctification, but receiving an archimedian rebound, which will ere long leap through pearly portals with shouts of victory, wing its flight from world to world, leaping over milky ways, chasing the planets in their orbits, the comets in their flight. With adoring wonder we are so delighted to wing our flight through trackless ether, unutterably electrified to do His will as the angels around His effulgent throne vie with each other, eternally progressing toward His blessed divinity, but never reaching it, as their sphere is angelic perfection, in contradistinction to our sanctification, with which we must be contented, till this mortal puts on immortality and glorification rushes in like a heavenly flood.

The second work of grace, constitutes entire sanctification, consisting of the complete expurgation of the heart by the cleansing blood applied by the Holy Ghost, when Jesus baptizes you, so not a vestige of depravity survives to antagonize the reign of grace in the heart; followed by His felicitous ingress. He fills you and floods you with the nine graces (Gal. 5:19), love, joy, peace, longsuffering, gentleness, goodness, faith, meekness, and holiness, which He pours out in your heart in regeneration and makes you perfect in sanctification by eliminating all antagonisms and giving you the constant victory over the world, carnality and Satan, thus lifting you up into the glorious hemisphere of a clean heart filled with the Holy Spirit and a life of constant sunshine.

Ezek. 47:1-12. Here we see the holy waters flowing out from the right-hand side of the altar; first ankle deep, then up to the knees, then to the loins, and finally over his head; waters to swim in. The reason why these holy waters flowed out from the right-hand side of the altar was because there the priests poured all the blood of the sacrifices.

When the Lord baptizes us with the Holy Ghost and fire, the Spirit, who is the custodian of the blood, applies it to the expurgation of inbred sin out of the heart and proceeds at once to come in, the blessed abiding comforter, the wonderful Parallyte, who not only condoles us amid all our sorrows, but makes life a glorious sunshine ringing out:

"I've reached the land of corn and wine,
And all its riches freely mine,
There shines undimmed one blissful day,
For all my sins have passed away.

My Savior comes and walks with me
And sweet communion here have we,
He gently leads me by the hand
For this is Heaven's border land.

A sweet perfume upon the breeze
Is borne from ever vernal trees,
Where flowers never fading glow
And streams of life forever flow.

The zephyr seems to float to me
Sweet songs of Heaven's melody,
While angels in their white-robed throng
Join in the sweet redemption song."

The negative hemisphere of sanctification, i. e.. the expurgation of depravity out of the heart by the

cleansing blood administered by the Holy Ghost
when Jesus baptizes you, is definite and complete;
the old man is crucified, the body of sin destroyed
so we no longer serve sin, actually buried into the
death of Christ, the grand and glorious vicarious
substitutionary atonement into which every sin personality, generated of fallen Adam, must be buried,
or it will find interment in a bottomless hell. Rom.
6:5-6. When the old man dies, he is dead all over
and forever, and the heart is clean, the Holy Spirit
filling it, giving victory so we neither sin in thought,
word or deed, but sing as we go:

"Oh happy bliss and joy sublime,
I've Jesus with me all the time.
I stand all bewildered with wonder,
And gaze on the ocean of love,
While over its waves to my spirit
Comes peace like a heavenly dove!

"The cross now covers my sins,
The past is all under the blood,
I am trusting in Jesus for all,
My will is the will of my God.

"I struggled and wrestled to win it,
    The blessing that setteth me free;
But when I had ceased from my struggles,
    His peace Jesus gave unto me.

"He laid His hand on me and blessed me,
    And bade me be every whit whole.
I touched but the hem of His garment
    And joy came thrilling my soul."

Whereas the negative hemisphere is complete when the sin personality is destroyed and removed by the wonderful efficacy of the cleansing blood, the positive is never finished, as you see clearly illustrated in this holy river, first to the ankles; then to the knees; still rising higher to the loin, and finally over head, a swelling ocean without bank or bottom. On it we lie prostrate, looking up to heaven, shouting the victory; thus moving on forever.

The reason why the people drown is because they turn their faces downward in the water and get strangled; whereas, if they were on the back the water would never overflow their faces and strangle them. This floating experience is unutterably delectable, moving in perfect harmony with God's providence and grace, jubilantly ringing one eternal yes to God and no to Satan; perfectly delighted with His sweet will, resting in His infallible promise, "All things work together for good to them that love the Lord." The holy river flowed out from the right-hand side of the altar where the priests always poured the blood of the sacrifices, symbolizing the blood of Christ which cleanses from all sin. 1 John 1:7. This brilliantly shows the negative side of the sanctified experience which crucifies the sin personality Rom. 6:6, buries his dead body in the atonement, raising the new man created by the Holy Ghost in the heart in regeneration, to walk in newness of life, shine and shout forever, jubilantly exultant in His wonderful freedom from the old body of sin (Rom. 7:22), which had encumbered him during all wilderness life. Now that he has crossed the Jordan into the land of Canaan, flowing with milk and honey and abounding in corn and wine, he is so happy he knows not what to do with himself; actually enjoying a glorious balloon ride with the Lord, soaring through the upper sky, and shouting till the angels hear him; feasting on a heavenly prelibation.

As the blood, applied by the Holy Spirit, when Jesus baptizes us expurgates away inbred sin, giving us a clean heart when He comes in to abide forever, making life one perennial day as all our night has passed away, actually giving us a heaven in which to go to heaven, where we sing incessantly.

My rapturous soul is sighing and crying night and day for the lost millions of earth, going to hell a sheer gratuity, as my wonderful Savior has already redeemed them by His blood, so freely shed on Calvary.

While the negative experience brought by the blood, administered by the Holy Ghost to the consecrated believing heart expurgates the depravity transmitted to every human being by Satan through fallen Adam, our federal head, thus giving us a clean heart which the Holy Spirit fills and the wonderful experience of entire sanctification; yet in the superabounding grace of God through the wonderful vicarious atonement which Jesus made on Calvary. The positive hemisphere legitimately follows, so brilliantly revealed by these holy waters Ezekiel saw flowing out from the right-hand side of the altar, where the blood had already procured the complete redemption and swelling to a copious river, up to the knees; then, to the loins, and then a swelling flood over his head, so he couldn't wade it any more, but found himself floating on the heaving bosom, far away till it became a mighty sea; broadening into an ocean, rolling eternally without bank or bottom.

Thus so signfiicantly it signifies the illimitable enlargement of this wonderful sanctified experience; the negative side by the cleansing blood, settling the sin problem forever and sweeping us out when Israel passed the flood of Jordan, entering the land of Canaan; delightful mansions they had never built, awaited the occupancy; wells of sparkling water they had never dug; vineyards loaded with luscious grapes they had never planted; figs, olives, pomegranate and endless diversities of most delicious, nutritious and hygienical fruit they had never planted; trees groaning under their copious crops and nothing to do but pluck the fruits, and eat to full satiety. Thus we have even in this probationary pilgrimage this wonderful gospel banquet; our Heavenly Father's table groaning under the fatted calf, floating in his own gravy and all the luscious fruits of Canaan; angel waiters all around us, giving summary attention and nothing to do but eat and grow into gianthood instead of abiding in pygmyhood. We lamentably recognize the popular churches all round us with magnificent edifices and beautiful furniture and everything heart could wish in the way of temporal outfit, but nothing to eat. The people dress like kings and queens, but have emaciated faces like ghosts, starving to death.

I was so delighted with the good providence which permitted me to visit the holy city, the light and joy of the whole world, but so surprised to find my books there, having out-traveled me. When I reached old dark India, how I was surprised to find my commentaries translated into the native languages and studied by those black, yellow, red and brown preachers of that far-off land. So traveling on I still found them in all parts of the world, even in dark Africa they are now extensively circulated. This is my two hundred and twenty-third, and the Lord has given me one hundred and fifty more whose names I have written down on the blank borders of my Greek Testament, and if He keeps me on the earth, I shall dictate them to an amanuensis and trust him to have them printed soon or late, as he willeth, even after I shall have exchanged the silver trumpet for the golden harp.

This glorious upper side of the sanctified experience is absolutely illimitable and will continue to broaden, deepen and tower into loftier altitudes, through the flight of eternal ages. A conclusion which follows as a legitimate sequence from the heavenly environments where everything is on our side and not an ounce of impediment; as we will never meet another Devil in all the flight of endless cycles; all the redeemed spirits, angels, archangels cherubims, seraphims and heavenly hierarchies with glorious and jubilant unanimity cheering us on; the heavenly arches ringing with shouts; copious volumes of hallelujahs rising and rolling through celestial vaults with ever increasing anthems of glory, honor, dominion and praise to Him who has loved us and given Himself for us. If we are faithful to the grace given, even in this world, we grow from babyhood into gianthood and make paradoxical proficiency in the divine life.

Amanda Smith, born in Southern slavery, with a knowledge of the alphabet, reached the front of the ministry, traveled around the world, honored to preach to the kings and queens of the Orient. I have preached alternately with her in the great camp meetings. If my ambition was not dead and I consequently wanted the pre-eminence, I would rather compete with the great men who honor the American pulpit, than Aunt Mandy. She held the multitudes spellbound by her wonderful eloquence and Pentecostal fire; that sable Ethiopian face, radiant with the celestial flame; multitudes thronging the altars, responding to her appeals.

There is no doubt but we grow in all the nine graces of the Spirit, through the flight of eternal cycles, forever approximating the Godhead but never reaching it. All finite beings are progressive, the good to profounder depths, broader latitudes, loftier altitudes and more agressive longitudes, while centuries, ages and cycles beat their march. The wicked, whether in this world or in hell, make a similar advancement retrogressively, sinking into profounder depths, a more terrible damnation, while endless cycles roll.

CHAPTER VII

GLORIFICATION

The blessed Holy Spirit, the executive of the Trinity, has three great works indispensible in our transformation from the Satanic to the Divine similitude. Regeneration for the sinner, sanctification for the Christian, and glorification for the saints when this mortal shall put on immortality. The latter, the subject of this chapter, we do not have to seek, as pursuant to His office He gives it in the article of death. As Satan brings into availability all the chicanery of hell on this wicked world to defeat all of these mighty works of the Holy Ghost, he stirs up people to seek glorification and has them to profess it, fallaceously, as no one can get it till this mortal puts on immortality.

I heard a man of three hundred pounds in a Cincinnati camp meeting tell his experience of conversion, sanctification and glorification to about a thousand people. I said, "Brethren, put this man on the scales and weigh him. If he has the weight of a feather, he is mistaken about his glorification, whose normal work is to eliminate all ponderous matter, so we will not weigh anything." The people laughed uproariously. That brother was in great danger of losing his sanctification, which, if not regained, would expose him to fearful liability of losing his justification and dropping into hell. You ask, "Can I lose my sanctification and retain my justification?" Certainly you can, as they are never both lost simultaneously. We do not lose sanctification by committing sin, but by the coming back of depravity, *i. e.*, by drinking it back into the heart."

While you are sanctified you can not commit a sin, because it is impossible to grow a crop without seed, which sanctification takes out of the heart, removing hereditary depravity, which is the Devil's seed corn, and without which he can not grow a crop. Therefore sanctified people never do commit sin till they have lost their sanctification by the reimbibition of depravity, *i. e.*, the evil spirits in the air manage to inject evil into your heart, so to your surprise you find yourself actually committing sin. If your sanctification had been on hand you would have died in your tracks rather than commit a known sin.

The Burning Bush people have notoriety for preaching this heresy of simultaneous forfeiture of justification and sanctification, which is simply the heresy of but one work of grace in salvation, which John Wesley in his debate with its author so refuted that he gave it up. History says he sought and found the second blessing and shouted up to heaven. What a pity that so many Methodist preachers are actually preaching that exploded heresy instead of the glorious truth of Wesleyan Methodism, now preached by all the Holiness people throughout the world.

Satan hates sanctification worse than anything else, because he knows that the people who get and keep it are gone out of his clutches world without end. Therefore he resorts to every device hell can hatch to keep people from getting it and then to cheat them out of it after they get it. That is the reason why he has the preachers preaching a third work of grace in salvation; in Yankee land, the blessing of power, quoting Acts 1:8, "You shall receive power after the Holy Ghost has come on you," is a wrong translation. The true reading, "You shall receive the power of the Holy Ghost having come on you," i. e., the Holy Ghost Himself is the power, and all we can ever get. Then the Devil says to sanctified people, you never can get any more, a lie to put them at a standstill when he knows he'll get them. Because sanctification mounts you on a bicycle to run for heaven, and if you try to stand still you fall down.

You received the Holy Ghost in sanctification but do not exhaust Him. You are very thirsty, you come to the Ohio river and take a drink, but you have not drunk up the river. Sanctification is an experience that will sweep on through the flight of eternal ages; first a limpid rill, leaping from the snow bank on the mountain summit; moving on, joined by tributaries till it becomes a swelling river, rolling in majesty, broader and deeper, till finally the Amazon, one hundred and fifty miles wide and a thousand feet deep, rolls into the Atlantic ocean.

Out of Egypt into Canaan there were two crossings—the Red Sea and the swelling Jordan. You know the retrogression from Canaan back into Egypt would require the same two crossings; over the Jordan into the Wilderness, and then the sea into Egyptian bondage. Hence you see clearly that the Burning Bush heresy is simply another name for the Zinzendorfian, which gave Wesley so much trouble, and he fought heroically, and actually saved its founder. But the Devil succeeded in holding it in the Methodist church, so I awfully fear this day, and verily believe, that the majority are not Methodist, but Zinzendorfians. Rest assured that you do not lose your sanctification by committing sin, from the simple fact that you can not commit it while you have a clean heart, as in that case the Devil would grow a crop without seed, which is an impossibility. The air is thronged with demons doing their best to put the depravity back in you and thus rob you of your purity. While both experiences are never lost simultaneously, they may come in so quick a succession that you will not differentiate between them. When the Burning Bush people were in their glory I followed them in Omaha, Neb., and Brother Dright, of that city, who had been gloriously converted and sanctified in Cincinnati camp (having been lassoed by the Bush and afterward saw his mistake, right about faced and is today a shining light) had hitherto entertained me and in his argument in favor of the Bush, gave me this case: "A man in this city, converted and sanctified, turns burglar, breaks in and robs, would he not lose both experiences?" I responded, "He would not lose either." The brother was surprised to think he could commit such a crime and lose neither his conversion nor sanctification when I proceeded to certify. When he yielded to the Devil, and consented to break into the store and commit the robbery he lost his justification, fell under condemnation, a miserable thief in the sight of God. Though the police caught him and prevented him from doing anything, or your burglar-proof locks (as he was traveling selling them) effectually defeated him, so to the eyes of the world he was the same innocent Christian. But in the sight of God he was a miserable, con-

demned rogue, hanging over hell by the brittle
thread of life."

He then said, "Did he not at the same time also
lose his sanctification?" I responded, "nay, verily,
if the Holy Ghost had been in his heart, as he dwells
in all sanctified people, he would have died in his
tracks rather than to consent to commit the crime."
History certifies that two hundred martyrs have in
bygone ages sealed their faith with their blood,
simply because they preferred to die than commit a
known sin, as everyone of them could in that way
escape death. Rest assured that no sanctified person ever does commit a sin (knowingly) because
Satan cannot grow a crop (and all actual sin is his
crop for the damnation of a soul). Therefore you
see that no one loses justification and sanctification
simultaneously. No one ever commits a known sin
while sanctified wholly and the Holy Spirit abiding
in the heart.

The second third blessing heresy was the baptism of fire Matt. 3:11. "He will baptize you with
the Holy Ghost and fire," a wrong translation, as
Satan founds all his heresies on statements which he
has managed to get into the Bible, as it reads, "He
will baptize you with the Holy Ghost and fire," the
second "with" not there. Eph. 4:5 tells us there is
only one baptism in salvation, and that Jesus gives
with the Holy Ghost and fire. I am invited to eat
dinner tomorrow with a saint of the Lord. I am
fond of cabbage and all other vegetables. If he gives
me bread and cabbage, I will be satisfied, and it will
not be two dinners, one bread and the other cabbage,
but only one dinner, consisting of bread and cabbage.

So Jesus gives one baptism, with the Holy Ghost and fire; the former applying the cleansing blood, and expurgating all depravity out of the heart, and the latter burning up styles, fashions, needless ornamentation, lodgery, tobacco, sectarianism, politics and all sorts of worldliness.

The third device of Satan against the Holiness people to cheat them out of their sanctification was the tongue movement, which is utterly false, as it is a well known fact that they have no tongue, as tongue means language, and they have nothing but noises like frogs and birds, imparted by the demons which throng the air (Eph. 2:1). They would give a language if they could in order to fool the people. Satan cannot give a language or he would, as he counterfeits everything God does, when it is in his power. Everybody can see for themselves that the Tongue people have no tongue nor baptism of the Holy Ghost, from the simple fact that so many of them, to our painful recognition, commit sins of all sorts. This is an impossibility with people who have the Baptism of the Holy Ghost, which has but one meaning in the Bible, and that is, the removal of depravity out of the heart, Luke 11:38, John 3:25, and many other passages.

Catharidzoo, which has no meaning but to purify, is the only definition of *baptidzoo* in the Bible, and simply means to take out of you everything the Devil put in you through the heredity of fallen Adam. Hence the fact that the Tongue people commit sin even while speaking in that demoniacal gibberish which they call a tongue. They are notorious for committing sin, and do not deny it, but confess outright sins horrific to mention. As I am acquainted throughout the United States and many countries, I know these sad facts to be true, and could give you a dark catalog confirmatory of the sad fact. This is really the confession of judgment against themselves, as it is an indisputable Bible truth that no one can enjoy the baptism and commit a sin, ever so small. All actual sin is the Devil's crop, which he cannot grow without the seed, which is the depravity of the heart, and the baptism of the Holy Ghost has no meaning in the Bible but its removal.

Oh, how we need Bible teachers in our pulpits everywhere, to fortify the people against Satan's counterfeit gospel preached by Tongue preachers, Mormon prophets, Campbellite preachers, Catholic priests and many backslidden preachers in the orthodox churches! That is the reason I am doing my best by speech and pen to stir out our sanctified people to preach the gospel, because the words of Jesus ring in my ears, "Pray ye, the Lord of the harvest that He may send forth laborers into His vineyard, the harvest is great and the reapers are few."

The gospel is regeneration for the sinner, and sanctification for the Christian, which are not doctrines, but experiences, which none can preach but those who have them. I preached the doctrine of sanctification fifteen years with all my might before the Lord gave it to me forty-nine years ago, and got nobody into the experience; from the simple fact that I myself did not have it. Jesus forbade his own apostles to go out preaching without the experience, but told them to tarry in Jerusalem, praying and seeking unil Pentecostal day was sent down from

CHERUBIM AND FLAMING SWORD

heaven, from the simple fact that they could not preach what they did not have.

That Messianic mandate is equally pertinent and forceful today. While Jesus restricts the ministry to those who have the experience, it is thrillingly imperative that all who have it, male and female (as He calls women as well as men to go and preach His gospel), should preach it. Oh, how we need all the people who have the blessed experience, regardless of sex, race, color, nationality or anything else, to go and proclaim the glad tiding of this wonderful salvation, so rich, sweet, full and free to the perishing millions. There are a thousand million heathen, three hundred million Mohammedans, four hundred and fifty million Catholics, as well as the lost myriads in the great Protestant churches, literally without salvation; the vast majority of the preachers without it, and consequently utterly incompetent to preach to others what they do not possess.

The Lord used my humble instrumentality to pioneer the Holiness Movement from the Atlantic to the Pacific. Meanwhile I met awful opposition everywhere, even mobbing me and threatening me with immediate death, but never scaring me off because I was ready to die, and I am now lost in the interest of God's kingdom, ready to preach and to die. If God were to give me a choice I would certainly turn it back to Him and beg Him to choose for me, as I might make a mistake and He cannot. I would shout over the privilege of reciprocating the favor He did me on Calvary. I would shout over the privilege of dying to save immortal souls, and God knows that if my martyrdom is more profitable to His kingdom than my ministry, at His infallible option.

A great Methodist preacher in Texas announced an appointment to refute my preaching, which he denounced as "North Fanaticism." An old slave had received it gloriously and he invited him to attend and give him a chance to knock the fanaticism out of him. Sure enough, when the great audience assembled, Ben looked down from the gallery, ready to hear his powerful sermon in which he electrified his carnal people by showing them there was no "second blessing," and they were alright without it. When he pronounced the benediction they thronged him with their congratulations on his wonderful success refuting the heresy which had troubled their consciences. Meanwhile Ben was looking on and he motioned to him to come in hearing distance, when he said, "Ben, how did you like the sermon?" The old slaves were always polite to their masters, so Ben responded, "Fine sermon, Boss." Then he said, "Well, I reckon you have given up your sanctification," when he said, "Oh, Boss, I said 'twas a fine sermon, but you did not go fur enuf." "What do you mean, Ben?" "Why, you said 'dere was no sanctification.' You should have said, 'not dat you nows of;' but I nows dere is for I'se got it. Glóry to God." The heavenly landslide flooded his soul and he shouted aloud, taking all the force out of the big sermon and they plainly saw that Ben had something that preacher knew nothing about.

Sanctification is the climax of all blessings in this life, and though beginning a tingling rill, broadens and deepens into a swelling river, magnifying into a majestic ocean without bank or bottom, normally in the article of death, crowned with glorification.

It is God's infallible passport, through the pearly portals into the new Jerusalem. Heb. 12:14.

Satan hates it so inveterately that he resorts to every conceivable strategem to cheat you out of it, running on you His fond caprices, cognomend *"third blessings,"* occult diabolical chicanery to get you away from it. Meanwhile he infuses depravity back into your heart, thus eclipsing the star of heavenly hope in the gloom of eternal night.

So all of these third blessings preached in the glorious plan of salvation, are satanic strategems to cheat people out of their sanctification, in that case He is sure to get them. Therefore his satanic majesty lays under contribution all hell and fallen earth thrown in for good count, in the first place, to keep people from getting sanctified; and in the second place to decoy them away from it and cheat them out of it, after they get it. In that magnitudinous enterprise, he has millions of preachers employed night and day. In their fond delusions vainly they congratulate themselves they are ministers of truth and righteousness, while clandestinely used by Satan for the population of hell, and the disappointment of heaven, whose omnipotent Son has already redeemed every soul by His precious blood.

Glorification is the grand climax of the restitutionary economy for which Jesus came into the world, launching His wonderful evangelism; regeneration rich and sweet, full and free for every sinner, even the vilest of the vile. It is on the solitary condition that he will leave the devil, world without end, giving him back all his sins, actual, original, hereditary, multitudinous infirmities, all sorts of mistakes and disconformities, and disharmonies with the divine administration, bidding him an eternal adieu. God with infinite delight cancels all hs condemnation from heaven's chancery, separating his sins far from him as the east from the west, actually burying them in the depths of the sea of forgetfulness, so they will never rise in the judgment to condemn us. Nor in the resurrection will they inundate us with shame when we leap into life immortal, responsively to the archangel's trumpet, join the blood-washed throng to sing the praises of redeeming grace and dying love forever. Thus His first great work, eternally sweeping away all condemnation, gives us a new heart and a new spirit (Ezek. 36:25) and the wonderful realization of Saul, the first king of Israel, when he met the Lord's prophets, and God gave him another heart and turned him into another man.

The second great work of the Holy Spirit is sanctification, which delivers us forever from the sin personality in all hearts hereditary from fallen Adam, our federal head. The very nature of Satan was so adroitly imparted to Adam and transmitted to everyone of his innumerable posterity, harmonically with the law of heredity, characteristic of all God's creation. In the first chapter in the Bible everything He created had its seed within itself, pre-eminently true of Adam, the climax of all creation; so constituted as to be competent to repeat himself infinitesimally, but could not transmit the divine life which he lost in the fall, and consequently could only fill the world with people minus the life, i. e., spiritually dead. Satan having not only robbed him of his spiritual life, but cunningly manipulated to substitute his own depravity, i. e., spiritual death, the prelude of endless damnation, superinducing the appalling metamorphism of the Edenic paradise into a hogpen, to fatten souls for the pandemonium.

In sanctification the blessed Holy Spirit applies the cleansing blood in the utter expurgation of that awful Satanic depravity which fills every heart generated of fallen Adam, superinducing the lamentable fact that every human being is conceived full of inbred sin. Ps. 51:5. "I was shapen in iniquity and in sin did my mother conceive me," sung by the Methodists round the world, "Lord, I am vile, conceived in sin, born unholy and unclean, sprung from the man whose guilty fall corrupts his race and ruins all." Satan in the Eden war achieved the greatest victory of the ages, because in Adam he seminally captured every human being through fugitive centuries, rolling ages, and illimitable cycles, revolved from fallen Adam. We are transcendently and gloriously rescued by our wonderful Christ. Heb. 2:9. "By the grace of God Christ tasted death for everyone."

Regeneration raises the soul from the dead, conquers inbred sin and gives grace to keep it down, involving us in a perpetual civil war and putting in the heart the perpetual cry for the victory over the world, flesh and Satan, for which we sigh and cry, "O wretched man that I am who shall deliver me from this body of death," Rom. 7:24. Paul in Arabia after seeking three years and availing himself of every conceivable faculty under the law and finding it utterly unavailable reaches desperation. This powerful historic illusion is to the ancient custom of taking a dead body from the battlefield, and tying it fast to each living captive; back to back, limb to limb, whereas the putrefaction exhaled from the corpse always killed the living soldier by an awful loathsome death, superinduced by the poisonous effluvia, if he did not have the good fortune to get loose from his awful pestilential burden. You see, the very moment he reaches desperation of all legalisms and churchisms, and turns the horrific dilemma over to the Omnipotent Savior, the victory comes instantaneously, revealed by his triumphant shout, "O thank God through Jesus Christ our Lord," gloriously confirming the maxim, "man's extremity, God's opportunity."

God has superaboundingly revealed the utter impossibility of admission into heaven without entire sanctification, Hebrews 12:14. We must at every cost go for it till we get it in an inundation of testimony, the bells of heaven ringing; from the crown of the head to the soles of the feet "sanctified holy." 1 Thess. 5:23. It absolutely sweeps all doubt beyond the north pole and confers on us the grand experimental certainty. We actually have in our hearts a prelibation of heaven, confirmatory of our personal citizenship. Phil. 3:20. "Our citizenship is in heaven, whence we are looking for our Savior, the Lord Jesus Christ, to appear and transfigure these mortal bodies simultaneously to His own glorious body. Really, this heavenly prelibation is the grand assurance and indubitable confirmation of our heavenly citizenship, beautifully involving the logical conclusion that every soul going to heaven takes his heaven with him in his heart, and every one going to hell takes with him the appalling prelude of his own damnation.

While regeneration gives the new heart and sanctification the clean heart, we still are full of infirmities, i. e., sins of ignorance, exposing us to the liability of doing wrong, aiming to do right. This does not bring condemnation nor disturb our peace, flowing like a river, yet it is incompatible with the heavenly state, which is on the basis of angelic perfection, which glorification the third great work of grace alone can confer. Sanctification from all inbred sin, polluting, following justification from all actual transgressions and freeing us from condemnation, constitutes the happy estate of the Christian in this world; every moment shouting the victory over the world, the flesh and Satan, electrified with a foretaste of coming glory. He stands on the delectable mountains with the telescopes of faith and hope, viewing the celestial city, with visions of angels on the wing, cheering him with the joyful "welcome home."

God alone has absolute perfection which we will eternally approximate, but never reach. The angels all enjoy a perfection which fortifies them against all mistakes and infirmities, and we actually reach it in glorification and fly away to heaven, flooded with angelic perfection in contradistinction from Christian perfection, which is the victory of the sanctified life. This grand third work of the Holy Spirit we never can reach "till this mortal shall put on immortality and mortality shall be swallowed up of life." I Cor. 15:51-60. It really not only delivers us from mortality, but materiality, rendering our bodies imponderable, i. e., so we do not weigh anything.

As our dispensation is on the high plane of entire sanctification, in contradistinction of its predecessor on the plane of justification, Jesus forbade His own apostles to preach till they received the experience, tarrying at Jerusalem and praying for it. He knew they could not preach what they did not have. It is astounding to see how the churches have ignored His infallible mandate, actually filling the world with unsanctified preachers, thus dragging down the gospel church from the lofty and triumphant heights of holiness, to the plane of premessianic ages and consequently impeding and paralyzing the victories of the cross in every land and nation, preaching a standard two thousand years behind the age.

If the church had rigidly adhered to our Savior's mandate, maintaining her ground on the plane of entire sanctification, she would have conquered the world long ago, ushering in the millenium with the glorified Savior reigning from Orient to Occident and from pole to pole. Regeneration and sanctification are not doctrines, but experiences, and consequently can not be preached by aliens. I preached fifteen years without the experience of sanctification, constantly emphasizing the doctrine, but could not preach the experience, from the simple fact that I did not have it. For this reason it is really imperative that all the people who enjoy these experiences should preach them to others, as they are the only hope of the lost world. Jesus has forever settled the problem, "Ye must be born from above," Jno. 3:7, and "without the sanctification no one shall see the Lord," Heb. 12:14. While education is all right in its place, it cannot make a preacher, from the simple fact that salvation is not educational, but experimental, actually restricting its propagation to its own possessor and qualifying all of them by the help of God to transmit it to others; pursuant to God's universal law proclaimed in the first chapter of the

Bible, that everything has its seed within itself and
is competent to repeat itself *ad infinitim*. Thus by
indefragable laws, forever tied up everything within
its own sphere, where infallible, Omniscient, Omnipotent and Omnipresent Jehovah launched it, when
worlds responsively to His mandate leaped from His
creative fingers and superseded chaos in their precipitated flight around the effulgent throne, evoking
the melodious songs of the morning stars, which
sang together while the sons of God all shouted for
joy.

I write about glorification, but am utterly incompetent to expound it, from the simple fact that I
have never received it and never can till this mortal
shall put on immortality, but we have the assurance
that it comes as a normal consequence of sanctification, the tree of life which produces the beautiful
and delicious fruit, angelic perfection, i. e., glorification. My oldest son went to heaven thirty-six
years ago in his twentieth year, while a student in
college preparing for a mission in China, where we
had so few missionaries at that time. He had been
joyfully converted at the age of eleven, sanctified in
his teens, and called to that distant heathen land to
preach the gospel to the children of the dark Orient,
sitting in the valley of the shadow of death.

Arriving home from an evangelistic tour our
family physician, accosting me on the street, said,
"Brother Godbey, your Jimmie will not live two
weeks as he has galloping consumption in its worst
form." One week from that day he leaped away to
heaven, while I was looking on his face at 10 a. m.
on a bright spring day. An unearthly radiance

dropped down from heaven, illuminating his physiognomy till it shone like a lamp, filling the room, thronged by Christian friends sympathizing with our sorrows. They were unutterably astonished in contemplation of the unearthly glory, flashing from his face and filling the room. The simple solution of this phenomenon is that the radiance was the normal splendor of the glorified soul, reflected on the vacated tenement as it evacuated the house of clay and soared away to its bright heavenly home beyond the glittering stars. We have often seen the king of days retreat behind the western horizon, at the same time lighting up the Orient with myriads of rainbow tints, red, orange, yellow, blue, indigo and violet, the sun's farewell to mother earth, and throwing back his valedictory kiss upon the eastern skies, magnetizing millions of eyes gazing with unutterable wonder.

When preaching in a Carolina city my attention was arrested by a phenomenon which impressed me as a city burning down, sinking under the fiery billows like an ocean of flame. I accosted a man who said that he was acquainted in that country and there was no city there. What was it? Simply the glory of the setting sun reflected from the evergreens, crags and precipices of the majestic mountain. I have often looked on the faces of the dead in their coffins, illuminated with this unearthful glory, the normal splendor of the disembodied soul reflecting the transcending beauty and glory of Him who assures us that we shall be like Him when He appears on a white cloud, accompanied by the glorified angels, to call away His waiting bride to the marriage supper of the Lamb.

When our Savior revealed His transfigured glory to Peter, James and John on the holy mountain, accompanied by Moses representing all who will be glorified through the resurrection, and Elijah, all who will be glorified through the transfiguration, the splendor eclipsed their mortal vision so they hid their eyes from the transcendent glory. When they opened them they saw Jesus only (Matt. 18:8), Moses and Elijah having retreated, thus beautifully symbolizing their delegated and receding power, superseded by the Prince of Glory. Thus He inaugurated the full orbed gospel day, whose glorious noon culminated in the Jerusalem Pentecost.

The present generation is the happiest of the ages, from the simple fact that all the chronologies vociferously proclaim His glorious coming to take away His bride, in cyclones of transfiguration glory, heralded by Gabriel's trumpet; in a moment, transformed out of materiality into spirituality, like Enoch, Elijah and John, "in the twinkling of an eye." (1 Cor. 15:51.) We shall leap up with shouts of victory climbing the skies, infinitely delighted to meet our varied kindred and loved ones from Abel down through the interesting centuries, gloriously resurrected, and infinitely delighted to meet the Lord in the air and be forever with Him. All shall go at once into the marriage supper of the Lamb, to respond to the roll call of the greatest ecumenical conference, saints, sages, and martyrs have ever dreamed, there to receive our appointments for the glorious millennial dispensation, everywhere ushering in. Satan is already arrested by the Apocalyptic Angel (Michael, I trow,) led away like a common criminal and imprisoned in hell a thousand years.

His myrmidons have skedaddled to the black regions of Erebus; the glory of the Lord floods the world, from sea to sea and pole to pole.

The glorification wrought by the Holy Ghost responsively to Gabriel's trumpet will bring back the bodies of all the saints slumbering in land and sea and simultaneously transfigure all the living members of the Bridehood. Thus they leap into the air with shouts of victory; climbing the azure firmament, flooded with rhapsody to meet Jesus descending on a white cloud, after which these glorified bodies will be the tenement of our glorified spirit forever, in contradistinction to the present life in which these bodies, like the animals all around, are the tenements of our own animal souls (the psychee). During our probation, we live like animals in these mortal tenements, but after the resurrection and rapture of the saints who will never die and need a resurrection, we will all occupy these identical bodies, glorified in the similitude of our Savior's body, which outshone the sun on the Mount of Transfiguration, and will shine forever illuminating celestial worlds. Meanwhile our bodies will radiate the same splendor and glory through all eternity.

This beautiful truth is confirmatory of the transporting assurance that the blessed Holy Spirit will glorify our sanctified spirits simultaneously with the evacuation of the body, thus sweeping away all the scars which have been left on the soul by the heavy tread of sin. The wounds were perfectly healed in sanctification, but the scars which mar the beauty of holiness were still left, superinducing multitudinous infirmities, mistakes, and blunders to the serious detriment of our magnetism for the glorification of Him who bled and died for us. These are all eliminated by the blessed Holy Spirit when He restores to us the pristine beauty and glory, our normal heritage, the concomitant of the divine image in which God created us. We will be eternally brightened with accumulated beauties, grandeurs and sublimities as we walk with our Heavenly Father eternally learning wisdom at His feet.

Oh, how transporting to contemplate this glorious restitution to the divine image undimmed by sorrow, unhurt by sin, to shine with every accumulating splendor through the flight of illimitable immortality. Our bodies, restored from mortality and materiality, homogeneous to our immortal spirit to the very similitude of God, will be utterly disencumbered of ponderosity. One hundred pounds now holds me on terra firma, and as Paul assures us (1 Cor. 15:51) it will come in the twinkling of an eye. The Omnipotent Holy Spirit instantaneously will glorify the sepulchred saints from Abel down to the trumpet blast of Gabriel who will descend with the Lord. 1 Thess. 4 ch. Then they will leap with shouts from land and sea throughout the inhabited earth; we who are alive meanwhile spellbound in contemplation of the unutterable glory filling the firmament. It will be as if a thousand suns had burst forth from worlds, shining in their majesty and beauty. We will instantaneously find ourselves flying with them far up in the lofty firmament, cities, rivers, seas and oceans far beneath our feet when we all together move in majestic throng to the marriage supper of the Lamb. There we shall receive our appointments in the grand and glorious holiness conference, preparatory to our delectable adminis-

tration subordinately to Christ, Rev. 6:20. "Blessed
and sanctified is he that hath part in the second
resurrection for over which the second death hath
no power for they bring presents unto God and
reign with Christ a thousand years."

CHAPTER VIII.

THE TREE OF LIFE RESTORED

Christ Himself is the Tree of Life of the Bible, the Flaming Sword, showing all honest inquiring souls the way to the Tree of Life. Through the long flight of the ages and dispensation we finally reach the millenial Armageddon. Satan's army goes down in signal defeat. Rev. 19. Pope and Mohammed are cast alive into the lake of fire in outer darkness, a thousand years before the devil gets there. King Diabolus, shaken down from his throne after a reign of six thousand years, will be arrested by Gabriel and led away like a common criminal and imprisoned in hell a thousand years.

Matt. 19:28. You who have followed in the regeneration shall sit upon twelve thrones judging, i. e., ruling the twelve tribes of Israel. Thus showing the fact the Apostles shall be first rulers of the world during millenium. Paul, doubtless, will be president of the United States, as we are his disciples (Acts 16:6-7), and he was traveling this way when he lost his head at Nero's block. Peter will be president of Britain; John of Russia, and the other nine the smaller kingdoms of the earth, as there are just about twelve great political dominions on the globe.

The millenium ingress will regenerate the earth; the great Armageddon, eliminating away all the incorrigibles and unsavables who must evanesce before the reign of righteousness, peace and joy can prevail on the earth. At the present day multiplied millions

need the military co-operated with the secular to
manage them. If the millenium were launched today, all of the policemen, armies, constables, sheriffs,
jails, penitentiaries and capital punishment would
be abolished.

The great work of the tribulation will be the
elimination of all the people out of the world unhar-
monizable with the millennial administration "of
righteousness, peace and joy in the Holy Ghost"
(Rom. 14:17) dispensed by the holiness preachers,
subordinate to our glorified Christ on the throne of
David in Jerusalem, Rev. 20:6. You see clearly that
there will be no government on the earth except a
pure holiness administration. Consequently the
millennium will be an utter impossibility with the
present population, dominating the whole world by
secular and military power, pre-eminently Satanic.

When a desperately wicked man, the terror of
the whole community, gets converted, his evil habits
are all slain by the two-edged sword, superinducing
a radical change, to the unutterable astonishment of
all his acquaintances. When I was a circuit rider
forty years ago, the Abraham of my parish related
his experience in love feast, stating that he had
plunged headlong into all the vulgar vices and
popular iniquities—nothing too vile for him. Coming home from a Satanic fandango at 1 p. m., his
attention is arrested by the vociferous prayers in
his father's negro cabin. Through curiosity he halts
and listens and finds that they are all praying for
their young master. Conviction like a thunderbolt
strikes him, knocking him down, when his melancholy wails arrest the attention of the godly Ethi-
opians, who rally around him, carry him into their

cabin, pray for him all night. With the rising sun
the glorious Son of Righteousness rises on his soul
with healing in His wings, giving him a new heart
and a new spirit (Ezek. 36:25). So he grabs those
ugly old negroes, hugging them affectionately, and
copiously kissing their black faces. He said they
shone like angels, and he actually thought them the
most beautiful people he ever saw.

The tribulation will kill off all the people who,
like the antediluvians in the days of Noah, the
Egyptians in the time of Moses, and the Jews who
rejected Christ, and were all destroyed by the flood,
the plagues, and the Roman armies; thus clearing
the track for the glorious ingress of a higher,
broader and more efficient dispensation of gospel
grace than the world had ever seen. Thus moves
on the grand conquest of our victorious Christ in the
indefatigable campaign for the restoration of this
world, back to the Edenic state of purity, beauty,
glory and immortality in which our blessed heavenly
Father launched it amid the shouts of all the angels
and the glorious heavenly jubilee.

As the regeneration of a wicked man kills off all
his evil habits, so the great Armageddon will destroy
all the people on the earth, who will not let God save
them; thus superinducing the regeneration of the
earth (Matt. 9:28), and indispensable concomitant
of the millennial ingress, so gloriously revealed, Isa.,
11th ch., "The cow and the bear will feed together,
the leopard lie down with the lamb, and the lion eat
straw like the ox; the infant will play at the hole of
the asp (moccasin, an awfully poisonous snake), and
the weaned child will delight itself at the den of
cocatrise (rattlesnake). God never created car-

nivorous animals nor poisonous reptiles, the deadly upas tree, the poisonous tobacco, nightshade lobia, monkshood, foxglove, etc.—all these Satan added after he conquered the world in the Eden war.

Therefore, when Satan's kings and queens all fall in the Armageddon (Rev., 19th ch.), himself arrested and imprisoned in hell (Rev. 20:1-3), and all his myrmidons skeedaddled from the earth, his power will so break through the world that even in her regeneration the carnivorous animals, as you see, will become grainivorous. The poisonous snakes will lose their venom, even the terrific rattler actually becoming a toy for the sportive infant, literally carried away with an automatic rattler.

While the millennial glory will inundate as the waters of the sea, "the nations having beat their swords into plowshares and their spears into scythes," so the generations will come and go; forgetting the awful rivers of blood and mountains of the slain, of the bygone ages turning mother earth into a graveyard, from the rising of the sun till the going down of the same. Yet the millennial will not be the final restitution, as it is only the regenerated state of the earth transitional to the glorious ultimatum which will be consummated when God shall rain fire down from heaven (Rev. 20:9), and burn up the devil's army, Gog and Magog, his copious gleaming from the greatest harvest hell ever reaped, i. e., the Armageddon. It will consist of the dynasties having encumbered all terrestial thrones, the six thousand years of Satan's reign, and finally heaped the battlefield with their carcasses (Rev., 19th ch.) ; their families reduced to plebeian rank and passing through the millennium. They will be magnetized by Satan's war toxin and drum beat, which had not been heard in a thousand years, beating for volunteers and promising the recovery of the thrones, crowns, and scepters enjoyed by their ancestors. Millionaires, railroad kings, big-bugs, high-fliers, upper-tens, "loving the pre-eminence," will rally under the sable banner of old King Diabolus, to fight for his re-enthronement as well as their own. Thus they coil round Jerusalem, by that time, as you see in Ezekiel, majestically built out over the great highlands of Palestine, Syria and Mesopotamia, a dozen times the magnitude of great London, the world's metropolis; so wonderfully built up by the imaginations of the Lord's saints of every land and clime, magnetized by the glorious reign of our blessed Christ on the throne of David in Jerusalem; the wonderful millennial prosperity throughout the whole world, superinducing finances so easy, money superabounding. At present $4.00 out of every $5.00 goes to the support of the armies and governments, leaving only one dollar out of every $5.00 for the laboring people to live on; whereas the ingress of the millennial will eternally sweep from the earth all human governments and armies with the exception of Satan's brief and abortive post-millennial campaign, ultimating in signal and hopeless defeat. The heavenly fires actually sweep his grand army into eternity (Rev. 20:9); expediting their final judgment which will eternally settle the doom of the devil and all his followers, demoniacal and human, precipitated into the lake of fire, *ies to nothos to exootion*, into the darkness which is without, *i. e.*, the darkness beyond the *ultima thule* of the illuminated universe. Everyone whose name is not found in the Lamb's Book of Life is precipitated into that lake of fire.

It is so infinitely distant that if an archangel moving with the velocity of lightning (Luke 10:18) had begun to fly on creation's morning he would not have passed over a millionth part of that space. Then how will Satan and his followers ever reach it! The omnipotent arm can transmit them thither in a twinkling of an eye, so infinitely distant as to preclude the possibility of ever getting back in all the flight of endless ages. Such is the appalling ultimatum of Satan and his myrmidons, and every human being who obstinately rejects the salvation Jesus has purchased with His own precious blood freely spilt on Calvary's cruel cross. Reader, be sure that you take no risk on this dismal and inevitable doom. The folly of standing in a rebellious attitude toward the divine administration climaxes all the colossal flights of human imagination. It not only means an eternity of woe, but actually a prelude of hell in this world, as there is no possibility of a happy moment, out of harmony with our Heavenly Father, who alone knows how to render us happy, and you may rest assured that He is delighted with the opportunity.

Our wonderful Father in His transcendent redemptive scene, through the atonement of His only Son, not only included the human spirit, the very similitude of God, the immortal intellect contradistinguishing us from the animal creation and the tenement in which we abide, but He even included Mother Earth, which He created for our home and gave to King Adam and Queen Eve, whom Satan dethroned, enslaving them and usurping their throne.

He will regenerate her in the millennial ingress
(Matt. 19:28), and sanctify her by the expurga-
torial fires (Rev. 20:9), which will not only utterly
consume Satan's post-millennial army; but burn out
everything Satan ever put in her.

The purgatorial baptism of the earth with the
Holy Ghost (Rev. 15:9) will burn out everything the
devil has ever put in her, as in the case of every
human soul in the glorious experience sanctification,
the divine *sine qua non,* without which no one shall
see the Lord (Heb. 12:14). When the great archangel Lucifer in heaven, a short time antecedently
to the creation of man, unfortunately supervened
when he yielded to ambition the greatest temptation
which predominated in the life of Sesostris, the Pharaoh on the throne of the world in Moses' time, and
the first man to subjugate the whole human race,
Nebuchadnezzar, Cyrus, Alexander the Great, Gen-
giskhan, Tamerlane, Hannibal and Bonaparte, who
aspired to the dominion of the whole world, reaching it through rivers of blood and mountains of the
slain. Thus Lucifer, having yielded to this ambition
to be a god instead of an archangel, and consequently
cast out of heaven, his influence drawing one-third
of all the angels (Rev. 1:4), who became demons;
the more criminal confined in the penal fires and
adamantine chains, while millions are permitted to
throng the air (Eph. 2:1), and tempt the people during our probation on the earth. In our journey
around the world we see it thronged with tramps,
in a state of nudity, or clothed with rags, fenced
with saloons, distilleries, brothels, penitentiaries,
tobacco fields and diversities of Satanic devices for
the destruction of soul and body; giving their poor

victims a hell on earth, an appalling prelude of the
endless misery awaiting the ungodly.

The flood only took out of the world the unsavables and incorrigibles, who had crossed the dead
line, despite faithful Noah's importunate preaching
120 years. The very same language is used in reference to the destruction of the world by water and
fire, and you see nothing was destroyed but the
reprobated people, who would not let God save them!
The Hebrew *nephilim,* from *anaphal,* to fall, and
consequently apostates. *Gibrim* translated giants,
not in the text, but simply the word which means
apostates, the normal fruit of the unhappy inter-
marriage of the righteous with the wicked, actually
ruining the antediluvian world and bringing on the
flood. This is an everlasting warning to all coming
generations, never under any circumstances to enter
into wedlock with the wicked, a risk God warns us
by the devouring flood never to run.

As you see the highest Biblical authority instead
of reading the earth and those things in it shall be
burned up. Simply means (shall be discovered),
therefore as we see (Rev. 20:9), only reveals the
destruction of the wicked Gog and Magog. Satan's
final remnant on the earth, leaving the teeming millions of holy people to verify our Lord's beatitude
(Matt. 5:5). The meek shall inherit the earth,
which will receive its happy fulfillment when the
fiery baptism shall eliminate everything Satanic,
actually sanctifying dear old Mother Earth, thoroughly revnovating and expurgating everything Satan ever injected into her organism. The purgatorial fires will melt and thoroughly purify the whole
world from all the pollutions of sin and iniquity, and

actually clear away all Satanic debris. It will transform her back into the Paradisian beauty, purity, and glory, which evoked all the shouts of all the angels, when in queenly majesty and splendor she wheeled out of shapeless chaos and took her place among her sister planets, unhurt by sin and undimmed by sorrow, to shine and shout around the effulgent Throne while the ceaseless cycles of eternity speed their flight.

Daniel 7:18, "I beheld, till the saints of the Most High, the kingdom will possess it forever and ever and ever." You see this Scripture actually proves the eternity of the earth. All the passages in King James relative to the end of the earth are translated erroneously and should read, "The end of the age." We are now treading the ragged edges of the Gentile age; the luna chronology, measuring by the revolutions of the moon around the earth, 354 days in the year, used by the patriarchs and prophets, Christ and his apostles, makes the Gentile age already expired, and seventy-one years more (1917), the calendar chronology, measured by the revolution of the planets around the sun, used in Europe, and by the apostle John, who saw all these prophetic visions on the Isle of Patmos, expires the Gentile times and sixteen years more. The solar chronology, used in America, and measures time by the revolution of the earth around the sun, 365 days in the year, gives us fifty-one years of Gentile time. As Daniel in his last chapter gives the tribulation forty-five years. (V. 12) 1,335 minus v. 11, 1,290 equals forty-five. As the tribulation is the last item in the Gentile dispensation, which began 587 B.C., and add 1917 A.D., equals 2,504, which is more than the whole. (Daniel,

4th ch.), 354 multiplied by 7 equals 2,478; whereas 2,504 minus 2,478 equals 26, plus 45, tribulation equals 71, showing up the fact that the rapture of the saints, which will take place immediately after the tribulation, is already overdue 71 years in luna chronology, while the calendar chronology, 360 multiplied by 7 equals 2,520, from which subtract the time already elapsed 2,504 equals 16, and subtracted from 45 equals 29, showing up the fact that calendar chronology makes the rapture of the saints overdue 29 years.

While our ^hronology, which has 365 multiplied by 7 equals 2,555, minus 2,054, the time already elapsed equals 51, and from it subtract Daniel's tribulation period 45, gives us 6 years, which will be 1,923. Hence, you see all the chronologies show up the fact that we are living in the time of the end when we should be on the constant outlook for His glorious appearing to take His waiting Bride.

It is pertinent to observe the significant fact that our Savior in His valedictory sermon on Mount Olivet Wednesday preceding His crucifixion says: "The tribulation will be shortened," otherwise no life would be left on the earth, the heavy artillery, gatling guns, torpedoes, submarines, dynamites, and especially the destroying angels (Dan. 7:9), a thousand thousand, *i. e., a* million.

No wonder no life would be left on the earth, but it is consolatory to hear Him say that tribulation will be shortened in the interest of the elect. Who are the elect? We answer, the people who will be left on the earth by the tribulation judgments, and will get saved in the millennium; the tribulation simply eliminating out of the world all the people who

will not let God save them. None survive but the
elect, who will hail the gospel. Millennial glory shall
flood the world as the water the sea (Rev. 19:23),
and (Acts 15:17), which if you will investigate
felicitously confirm the cheering conclusion that all
the people who survive the tribulation will jubilantly
turn to God with shouts of victory when millennial
glory inundates the earth as the water the sea.

N. B.—God is not tied to chronologies, as they
are for us to post us up so that we will be on the
lookout for His glorious appeai.... night and day,
"robed and ready with loins girded; staff in hand,
lamps trimmed and brightly burning like people
waiting for their Lord, responsively to the trumpet
blast, to go out to meet Him with shouts of victory.

We have the present war. Rev. 16:13-14, "I saw
three unclean spirits come out of the mouth of the
beast, the dragon and the false prophet, i. e., Catholicism, Paganism, and Mohammedanism. They will
go forth to stir up the kings from the rising sun to
the great battle of the God Almighty, which is Armageddon.

It is a significant fact this war was not born of
national animosities and perturbation. The nations
involved were all united in peace conferences, congratulating themselves that the world would never
see another war, as by their wisdom and philan-
thropy they could effectually head them all off. Suddenly a fracas broke out among some of the crowned
heads which they should have settled peacefully and
by arbitration. But suddenly they simultaneously
began to march off to the battlefield, demonstrating
the demoniacal intervention. The very next verse

(15) gives us the Rapture of the saints, "Behold, I come as a thief, blessed is he that keepeth his garment, that he may not walk naked and they shall see his shame."

Our Savior is only coming for His Bride, including all the wise virgins, who have not only their lamps lighted in regeneration, but filled with oil in sanctification, and consequently robed and ready, watching and waiting for His glorious appearing; ready to raise the shout, and to go out to meet Him in unutterable delight. The foolish virgins, so denominated because they took the Zinzendorfian view, which so many are preaching that the one work of grace is sufficient, in counter distinction to their wise comrades who soliloquized, "We know not how long the Bridegroom will tarry, how dark the forest, scalrous the moutains, dreary the deserts, flooded the rivers, through which we must travel," and consequently they all proceed to have their vessels filled with oil, i. e., hearts filled with the Holy Ghost which is the glorious second work our Savior gives all the children of God when He baptizes them with the Holy Ghost and fire. He is the Custodian of the blood, Heaven's Laundryman, who faithfully applies the blood, the omnipotent elixir of purification.

He perfectly expurgates every stain and making the heart whiter than the snow, as Paul in his Epistles so frequently uses that strong Greek compound, *eilekirina,* from *eilee,* a sunbeam, and *krinoo,* to judge. This signifies the consolatory assurance that the blood of Jesus so perfectly purifies the heart, that when illuminated with the great Son of Righteousness Gods' omniscient eyes signally fails to find any impurity. It evokes the exclamation of saints and angels *"mirable dictu,"* wonderful to tell, thus constituting the theme of the swelling *gandeamus,* which will roar and reverberate through heavenly arches, while centuries, ages, and cycles speed their precipitate flight. Meanwhile the sacramental hosts of the redeemed rend celestial vaults with their shouts, "victory, honor, dominion, and glory to Him who hath loved us and given Himself for us."

Will there be any chance for the foolish virgins and the sinners who will be the only people left on the earth when the Lord takes up His Bride? You find the answer, Rev. 20:4, "I saw thrones and those who sit on them and the souls of those who had been beheaded for the witness of Jesus, who had not worshipped the beast nor his image nor received his mark on their foreheads." The tribulation will set in immediately after the rapture of the saints, when antichrist, *i. e.,* the pope (Rev., 17th ch), will take the throne of the world, and require everybody to recognize his supremacy, *i. e., to* worship the beast and receive his badges.

The Rapture of the saints will stir the world as never before in all bygone ages. Newspapers will electrify every nation and give it universal publicity; the people crowding their churches and clamoring to their pastors, "You have ruined us by your reticence, permitting us to miss the opportunity of our lives of which the Holiness people gave us ample warning. They sang day by day, 'Some morning fair we are going away and will not come back till millennial day.' Now they are gone and we are left to the awful doom of the great tribulation of which Daniel and John so faithfully warned us." They plead with them, their tears flowing, "Do

forgive us as we were led astray by our presiding
elders and bishops. But there is still a chance as
God's mercy endureth forever." Oh, how they crowd
the altar and pray on all night when the people
clamor to their Catholic officers to suppress the dis-
turbance, but they signally fail, as these convicted
people see that if they obey the pope it simply means
damnation.

History gives the pope's martyrs who have already sealed their faith with their blood, a mini-
mum of 50,000,000 and maximum of 100,000,000.
You see (Rev. 5:9) the souls of those who had been
beheaded, for the witness of Jesus under the altar
crying for vindication when the answer comes, "You
must wait till your brethren who shall be beheaded
are added to you." This shows up the fact that the
tribulation martyrs have still to come in.

You see Jesus has held His grand Holiness conference during the Marriage Supper of the Lamb
and given all the saints their appointments for the
oncoming millennial reign. He now comes down to
establish His kingdom on all the earth. He resur-
rects the tribulation martyrs, and gives them all appointments, so that they will be members of the
Bridehood blest with the supplement to the first
resurrection. This took place when Gabriel blew his
first trumpet, and all the buried saints leaped into
life, and the living instantaneously transfigured (1
Cor. 15:21), were caught up with them to meet the
Lord in the air.

While these tribulation saints all have their heads
cut off, and are honored with a supplement of the
first resurrection, they utterly miss the Marriage
Supper of the Lamb and suffer the awful persecu-

tions of the tribulation, even having their heads cut off. Hence you see the pertinency of the grand desideratum and have a place in the rapture of the saints.

While the tribulation will be memorable for the awful judgments of God against the wicked nations and fallen churches, heaping the earth with mountains of the slain and deluging the nations with rivers of blood; it will also be celebrated in the annals of the ages. For tribulation revivals will sanctify the foolish virgins as well as convert and sanctify those sinners who have the heroism to suffer martyrdom in order to be true to God; thus losing their heads to save their souls, actually gaining a place in the Bridehood, as the Lord raises from the dead all who had been decapitated during the tribulation.

We see the doxology of that wonderful Pauline prayer, Eph. 3:14-21, "Now unto Him who is able to do exceedingly by above all we ask or think according to His own dynamite which worketh in Him, be honor, glory, dominion, and power unto all generations of the ages. It is impossible to have generations without birth.

N. B.—The commandment, "Multiply and fill the earth," was given to Adam and Eve before the fall. If Satan had let us alone humanity would have multiplied in purity and holiness and thronged the world with the happy multitudes, shining and shouting in the image of God. As Jesus was made "manifest to destroy the works of the devil," and is sure to do it; the sanctification of the earth by fire (Rev. 20:9) will eliminate everything belonging to the devil, as in case of the human soul, when Jesus baptizes us the blood expiates all Satanic depravity, making us meek and lowly like Jesus, going about doing good.

You see the last two chapters in the Bible give us a brilliant panorama of the renewed earth having risen from the ruins of our own conflagration, brighter than Eden ever shown, and reannexed back to Heaven. She moved in splendor, beauty, and glory around the effulgent throne, singing and shouting the praises of Him whose creative hand had given her a place among the multiplied millions of revolving worlds. Satan when precipitated in the heavenly altitudes (Rev., 12th ch.), caught her in his fall, determined to make her a valued accession to his dominions, and indefatigable hell feeder; a prolific hogpen to fatten souls for the barbecues of the pandemonium. As the millennial is the last dispensation in the restitutionary economy, regenerated in her ingress, Matt. 19:28, and sanctified gloriously in her egress, Rev. 20:9. When her baptismal fires will burn up Gog and Magog, the finale of Satan's kingdom on the earth and literally melt the earth and eliminate all Satanic debris, making her pure and holy as she bloomed on Eden's bright morn.

Meanwhile we see the new Jerusalem, the Bride of Christ, the mother of us all (Gal., 4th ch.) now metamorphosed into a city, and coming down from God out of heaven, the glorious synonym of entire sanctification. Her length, breadth, and height are all equal; brilliantly illustrating the sanctified soul, all O. K. in any position or attitude, knocked down, turned over. It is like the cat, dropped with its back down, but always lighting on its feet; so the sanctified soul always and everywhere is ready to preach and to die, singing night and day:

"Oh matchless bliss and joy sublime,
  I have Jesus with me all the time.
  My Jesus, I love Thee,
  I know Thou art mine.
  For Thee all the follies of sin I resign;
  My blessed Redeemer, my Savior art Thou,
  If ever I loved Thee,
  My Jesus, 'tis now.
  I love Thee because Thou hast first loved me,
  And purchased my pardon on Calvary's tree;
  I love Thee for wearing the thorns on Thy brow.
  If ever I loved Thee, my Jesus, 'tis now.
  In mansions of glory, in endless delight,
  I'll ever adore Thee in yon heaven of light;
  I'll sing with the glittering crown on my brow.
  If everl I loved Thee, my Jesus, 'tis now."

Brother Godbey, as you say when the fires sanctify the earth, destroying Gog and Magog, Satan's remnant (Rev. 20:9), and the meek, i. e., the holy people, shall sanctify the whole earth and the holy people possess it forever and ever (Dan. 7:18), and the original Edenic economy, multiplying the people, the result will be an over-population. I made a calculation of the oceanic bottom and found the Pacific 70,000,000,000 acres, the Indian 19,000,000,000, and the Atlantic 16,0000,000,000, equal 107,000,000,000 acres. Now divide it into farms of 1,000 acres, and you will have 105,000,000 acres, amply sufficient for 100 people on each; giving us a population of 10,500,-000,000 inhabiting the oceanic beds, as we are assured there will be no more sea, as the fiery baptism will have consumed them all, thus adding their fertile beds to the table earth.

Besides you must remember that if Satan had let us alone nobody would ever have died, but at the end of probation, guided by instinct of providence having access to the tree of life, the normal effect of whose fruit eliminating all ponderous matter and transfiguring our bodies so we would all have flown away with infinite delight, winning our flight from world to world, unutterably delighted to do our heavenly Father's will as the angels do it in heaven.

You see (Gen. 22:1) the tree of life which bloomed in Eden during the dispensation of innocency, restored back, brilliantly conformitory of our Savior's glorious and eternal victory over the devil. It not only supplies the fruit competent to metamorphose our bodies out of materiality into spirituality, but the leaves are ample and eternal fortification against all bodily ailments ever again coming on the earth. Thus you see the Bible winding up with the devil's utter and eternal defeat, with all his followers, demoniacal and human, banished eternally into the lake of fire (Rev. 20:15), infinitely far away in "outer darkness," i. e., so infinitely distant that the combined illuminations of 200,000,000 of glowing suns have never reached it with a cheering ray.

As earth is the battlefield of God's universe where His sons met the devil and all the hosts of hell fought, bled and died; so perfectly satisfying the violated law as to preclude the vaguest apology for the damnation of a solitary soul, and gloriously consummating the restitution of this earth back to Edenic beauty, purity and glory in which His holy inhabitants will shine and shout forever. Our triumphant Adam the Second having superseded Adam the First in the federal headship of the race, super-inducing the glorious fulfillment of Isaiah, "It will no longer be said that the parents had eaten sour grapes and the children's teeth thereby set on edge." Thus involving the beatific assurance that even the heredity which Satan entailed upon us will be glori-,ously eliminated and the days of primitive innocency restored.

N. B.—The work of Christ will not only ultimate in the restoration of this lost world, but gloriously superinduce the confirmation of all other worlds; thus giving the boundless celestial universe the benefit of the victories so gloriously achieved on Calvary. In the divine economy we will wing our flight from world to world, everywhere preaching divine loyalty, joyful obedience and loving conservatism to the felicitous administration of Father, Son, and Holy Ghost throughout the illimitable magnitude of God's wonderful celestial universe. Now to the dear Holiness people of all nationalities, regardless of race, color, nationality, sect, denomination, kindred, blood, and tongue, this book with its 222 predecessors is lovingly dedicated, praying the Father, Son, and Holy Ghost to make it a blessing to the dear saints of every land and through them to all the sinners.   W. B. GODBEY.

www.ingramcontent.com/pod-product-compliance
Lightning Source LLC
Chambersburg PA
CBHW021153020426
42331CB00003B/45